C000228473

THE GRID

	Defini-tory Hypo-theses 1	ψ 2	Nota-tion 3	Atten-tion 4	Inquiry 5	Action 6	. . . n.
A β-elements	A1	A2				A6	
B α-elements	B1	B2	B3	B4	B5	B6	. . . Bn
C Dream Thoughts Dreams, Myths	C1	C2	C3	C4	C5	C6	. . . Cn
D Pre-conception	D1	D2	D3	D4	D5	D6	. . . Dn
E Conception	E1	E2	E3	E4	E5	E6	. . . En
F Concept	F1	F2	F3	F4	F5	F6	. . . Fn
G Scientific Deductive System		G2					
H Algebraic Calculus							

Related Titles

LEARNING FROM EXPERIENCE

BY

W. R. BION,

D.S.O., B.A., M.R.C.S., L.R.C.P.

MARESFIELD LIBRARY
LONDON

First published in 1962 by
William Heinemann Medical Books Ltd.
Reprinted 1984 with permission
of Francesca Bion by
H. Karnac (Books) Ltd.
58 Gloucester Road,
London S.W.7.,
England

Second printing 1988
Third printing 1991

Printed in Great Britain by BPC Wheatons Ltd, Exeter

ISBN 0 946439 05 2

ACKNOWLEDGMENTS

Some of those to whom I am indebted I know, and to them I can acknowledge my debt. I am aware of others, notably patients, on whose cooperation I have always to depend, but who must remain anonymous. Dr. Elliott Jaques, Mr. R. Money-Kyrle and Dr. H. Segal have helped by reading and criticizing my manuscript. Just what generosity of time and effort this means for practising psycho-analysts can only be appreciated by another practising analyst.

Finally, as always, there is my debt to my wife without whose support I could not attempt to write at all.

ACKNOWLEDGMENTS

INTRODUCTION

1. As THE PROBLEMS raised in this book are fundamental to learning they have a long history of investigation and discussion. In psycho-analytical practice, particularly with patients displaying symptoms of disorders of thought, it becomes clear that psycho-analysis has added a dimension to the problems if not to their solution.

2. This book deals with emotional experiences that are directly related both to theories of knowledge and to clinical psycho-analysis, and that in the most practical manner. The man trained in philosophical method does not usually have the analyst's intimate experience of disturbed thought processes, and even psycho-analysts rarely undertake such cases. I have been fortunate in this respect, but lack the philosopher's training. I have however had the advantage of having undergone an analysis first with John Rickman and then with Melanie Klein.

3. I have experience to record, but how to communicate this experience to others I am in doubt; this book explains why. For a time I thought of concentrating on analysis of trainees. I am confident that psycho-analysts are right in thinking that this is the only really effective method of passing on analytic experience that we have at present; but to limit one's energies to this activity smacks of the esoteric cult. On the other hand, publication of a book, such as this, may seem premature. Nevertheless I believe it may be possible to give some idea of the world that is revealed by the attempt to understand our understanding. If the reader is tempted to go further the object of the book is achieved.

4. I have kept notes and references down to the minimum; they are essential to thinking the thought through rather

than merely reading the book. The book is designed to be read straight through once without checking at parts that might be obscure at first. Some obscurities are due to the impossibility of writing without pre-supposing familiarity with some aspect of a problem that is only worked on later. If the reader will read straight through, these points will become clearer as he proceeds. Unfortunately obscurities also exist because of my inability to make them clearer. The reader may find the effort to clarify these for himself is rewarding and not simply work that has been forced on him because I have not done it myself.

5. It may seem that I am mis-using words with an established meaning, as in my use of the terms function and factors. A critic has pointed out to me that the terms are used ambiguously and the sophisticated reader may be misled by the association of both words with mathematics and philosophy. I have deliberately used them because of the association, and I wish the ambiguity to remain. I want the reader to be reminded of mathematics, philosophy and common usage, because a characteristic of the human mind I am discussing may develop in such a way that it is seen at a later stage to be classifiable under those headings—and others. Nevertheless I am not discussing whatever it is that the function may become; my use of the term is intended to indicate that whether the person observed is performing a mathematical calculation, a walk with a peculiar gait, or an envious act all are for me functions of the personality. If I concern myself with the accuracy of his mathematics it is not because I am interested in his mathematics but because his mathematics, and the accuracy of his performance, are functions of his personality and I want to know what the factors are.

6. If the reader will consider the previous paragraph (5) again he will see that by claiming the use of the term function and wishing it to retain its penumbra of associations I leave it to be supposed that the term will be used by me in accordance with the rules and conventions by which mathematicians and philosophers regulate its use. If I fulfil this expectation I may be thought to use the term

"properly". But if I disappoint the expectation (aroused by the penumbra of associations of which I do not divest it) I may reasonably be said to mis-use the term. It is then open to me, if I agree with the criticism, either explicitly to divest the term of its penumbra of associations, or, to accept the conventions of use implied by its associations.

7. In fact I wish to follow neither course. Suppose I see the man walking. I may say that his walk is a function of his personality and that I find, after investigation, that the factors of this function are his love for a girl and his envy of her friend. Or that the factors in this function are his love for the girl and his envy of her friend. After further investigation I may decide that to his love for the girl is added envy of her friend; or F (his gait) $= L + E$. (F $=$ function, L $=$ love, E $=$ envy). But I may feel that my observations approximate to the Kleinian theory of projective identification and that I can express my opinion of the facts best by saying the function walking is a sign that the patient feels he has taken into him a loved girl with whom he is identified and a rival of whom he is envious but with whom he has also identified himself, and that both objects are controlled by being enclosed in his legs. I shall spare the reader a geometrical figure, expressing this last idea "mathematically"; but will ask him to consider whether in Chapter I the terms "function" and "factor" are mis-used. I understand that the use can confuse but cannot agree that it can be decisively declared to be mis-use. In a later chapter I claim that the use of ideas, and the symbols representing them, is less advanced than the process by which ideas are evolved. For this reason I am prepared to believe I am mis-using an idea, or its symbol, or both, but I am not prepared to agree that there is yet a definitive criterion by which the matter can be decided. In psycho-analytic methodology the criterion cannot be whether a particular usage is right or wrong, meaningful or verifiable, but whether it does, or does not, promote development.

8. I do not suggest that promotion of development provides a criterion without reservation; psycho-analytic theory and practice, in cases where thought shows serious disturbance,

indicate the need for a reformulation of ideas about the origin and nature of thoughts and a parallel reformulation of ideas about the mechanisms by which "thinking" thoughts is achieved. But if it is necessary to change our views about thoughts and the mechanisms of thinking it is likely that the change of views, if it is as significant as I think, will require modification of the way in which we produce "thoughts" and the methods we employ in using them. My method of producing "factor" and "function" (and their fitness to represent a realization) is not necessarily wrong because it is different from methods ordinarily accepted as conformable with the proper production, nature and use of concepts, but my method is not therefore exempted by the critical scrutiny to which I consider all thinking needs to be subjected in the light of psycho-analytic experience.

9. The methods in this book are not definitive. Even when I have been aware that they are inadequate I have often not been able to better them. I have found myself in a similar position to the scientist who continues to employ a theory that he knows to be faulty because a better one has not been discovered to replace it.

Summary of Contents

The following plan of the book may serve as a rough guide:
Chapter 1 embodies a preliminary explanation of two terms.

Chapter 2 is a demarcation of area in which I wish to use the terms as part of my equipment of inquiry.

Chapter 3 commences a stylized description of emotional experiences, realizations, in which I have participated, that form the stimulus for the whole of this book. By "stylized" I mean that it is consciously sophisticated because the falsification that is introduced by such a method of presentation is immeasurably less than the falsification produced by any others, including so called mechanical recordings. These last have the truth that pertains to a photograph, but the making of such a record, despite a superficial accuracy of result, has forced the falsification further back—that is into the session itself. The photograph of the fountain of truth may be well enough, but it is of the fountain after it has been muddied by the photographer and his apparatus; in any case the problem of interpreting the photograph remains. The falsification by the recording is the greater because it gives verisimilitude to what has already been falsified.

Chapter 4 is a brief statement of some of the ideas that are discussed throughout this book.

Chapters 5–11 are a summary description of clinical phenomena related to the subject matter of the book; these are familiar to analysts but couched in terms that are probably more meaningful to analysts trained in Kleinian theories. The description indicates the use to which I put the term **alpha-function and contact-barrier and at the end of Chapter**

11 I draw attention to the importance of the choice between modifying frustration and evading it.

Chapter 12 commences with a discussion of projective identification and its bearing on the genesis of thought. The subject leads on to the part played by oral and alimentary experience in providing a model for thinking. I draw attention to the serious consequences for development of a mother incapable of reverie.

Chapter 13 deals with problems of recording sessions and the theories used by the analyst, and discusses possibilities that offer an approach to a method of scientific notation in Chapter 14.

Chapters 14–16 introduce the signs L, H, and K, for use in the discussion of the matter of this book.

Chapters 17–18 return to the use of the abstraction "alpha-function" for discussing the genesis of thoughts. The problems of abstraction or generalization and concretization or particularization are then discussed.

Chapter 19 starts the discussion of the use of psychoanalytical models.

Chapter 20 is an investigation of abstraction in which an attempt is made at using abstract signs to elucidate some of the problems of abstraction as they present themselves in analysis.

Chapter 21 introduces the Kleinian theory of interchange between depressive and paranoid-schizoid positions: its relationship to learning and the emotional experience associated with the terms employed in theories of causation is explored.

Chapters 22–23 discuss model making and abstraction in the context of analytical practice.

Chapters 24–27 continue the explanation with particular reference to learning (K link). Chapter 28 is an elaboration of the same theme in minus K ($-$ K).

CHAPTER ONE

1. To CALL AN ACTION by the name of the person of whom it is thought to be typical, to talk, for example, of a Spoonerism as if it were a function of the personality of an individual called Spooner, is quite usual in conversation. I take advantage of this usage to derive a theory of functions that will stand up to more rigorous use than that for which the conversational phrase is employed. I shall suppose that there are factors in the personality that combine to produce stable entities which I call functions of the personality. The meaning that I attach to the terms "factors" and "functions" and the use to which I put them will presently appear, but some preliminary explanation may not be amiss.

2. The statement "A factor in X's personality of which we shall have to take account is his envy of his associates" is one any layman might make and may mean little or much; its value depends on our estimate of the person who makes it and of the weight he attaches to his own words. The force of the statement is affected if I attach to the term "envy" the weight and meaning with which it has been invested by Mrs. Klein.

3. Suppose now another statement: "X's relationship with his associates is typical of a personality in which envy is a factor." This statement expresses the observation of a function, the factors in which are transference and envy. What is observed is not the transference or envy, but something that is a function of transference and envy. It is necessary, as a psycho-analysis proceeds, to deduce new factors from the changes observed in the function and to distinguish different functions.

4. "Function" is the name for the mental activity proper

to a number of factors operating in consort. "Factor" is the name for a mental activity operating in consort with other mental activities to constitute a function. Factors are deducible from observation of the functions of which they, in consort with each other, are a part. They can be theories or the realities the theories represent. They may appear to be commonplaces of ordinary insight; they are not because the word used to name the factor is employed scientifically and therefore more rigorously than is usual in conversational English. Factors are deduced not directly but by observation of functions.

5. The theory of functions makes it easier to match the realization[1] with the deductive system[2] that represents it. Moreover, its use gives flexibility to an analytical theory, that may have to be used in a wide variety of analytical situations, without impairing the permanence and stability of the structure of which it is a part. Furthermore, by virtue of the theory of functions deductive systems possessing a high degree of generalization can be seen to represent observations in the analysis of a particular patient. Since psycho-analytic theory has to be applied to the changes occurring in the personality of the patient this is important. If the analyst observes functions and deduces the related factors from them, the gap between theory and observation can be bridged without the elaboration of new and possibly misguided theories.

6. The function I am about to discuss for its intrinsic importance also serves to illustrate the use to which a theory of functions can be put. I call this function an alpha-function so that I may talk about it without being restricted, as I would be if I used a more meaningful term, by an existing penumbra of associations. By contrast, the meaning of theories that appear as factors must be preserved and employed as rigorously as possible. I assume that the meaning has been made sufficiently clear by the authors and others who have discussed the theories with critical sympathy. The freedom implicit in the use of the term alpha-function and the concentration of precision of expression and employment into all that pertains to the factors,

confers flexibility without impairing structure. The use I make of an existing theory may seem to distort the author's meaning; if I think so I have acknowledged it, but otherwise it is to be assumed that I believe I am interpreting the author's theory correctly.

7. The term alpha-function is, intentionally, devoid of meaning. Before I indicate the area of investigation in which I propose to employ it, I must discuss one of the problems incidental to this investigation. Since the object of this meaningless term is to provide psycho-analytic investigation with a counterpart of the mathematicians variable, an unknown that can be invested with a value when its use has helped to determine what that value is, it is important that it should not be prematurely used to convey meanings, for the premature meanings may be precisely those that it is essential to exclude. Yet the mere fact that the term alpha-function is to be employed in a particular investigation inevitably leads to its reinvestment with meanings derived from the investigations that have already been carried out in that field.[1] Constant vigilance must therefore be exerted to prevent this development or the value of the instrument is impaired at the outset. The area of investigation is approximately that covered by the writings described in my next chapter.

CHAPTER TWO

1. DESCRIBING THE INSTITUTION of the reality principle Freud said, "The increased significance of external reality heightened the significance also of the sense-organs directed towards that outer world, and of the consciousness attached to them; the latter now learned to comprehend the qualities of sense in addition to the qualities of pleasure and pain which hitherto had alone been of interest to it." I emphasize, "the latter now learned to comprehend"; by "the latter" Freud presumably means "the consciousness attached to the sense impressions".[1] The attribution of comprehension to consciousness I discuss later. Of immediate concern is the function of comprehension itself; comprehension of the sense impressions and comprehension of the qualities of pleasure and pain are both investigated in this discussion. I treat sense impressions, pleasure and pain as alike real, thereby discarding the distinction that Freud makes between the "outer-world" and pleasure and pain, as irrelevant to the theme of comprehension. I shall however discuss the bearing of the Pleasure principle and the Reality principle on the choice that a patient can be seen to make between modifying frustration and evading it.

2. The attribution of comprehension to consciousness leads to contradictions which are avoided by accepting, for purposes of the theory I wish to propound, Freud's later conceptualization, "but what part is there left to be played in our scheme of consciousness, which was once so omnipotent and hid all else from view? *Only that of a sense-organ for the perception of psychical qualities*". (Freud's italics.)

3. Continuing the quotation from Freud's Two Principles of Mental Functioning "A special function was instituted

4

which had periodically to search the other world in order
that its data might be already familiar if an urgent inner need
should arise; this function was *attention*. Its activity meets
the sense impressions half-way instead of awaiting their
appearance."[1] Freud did not carry his investigation of
attention far, but the term, as he uses it, has a meaning I
would investigate as a factor in alpha-function.

4. To continue, "At the same time there was probably
introduced a system of notation, whose task was to deposit
the results of this periodical activity of consciousness—a part
of that which we call memory." Notation and the deposition
of the results of attention are also phenomena to be investigated by the aid of the theory of alpha-function.

5. Certain theories of Melanie Klein and her co-workers
will be considered; I list them here. They are: Splitting
and projective identification[1]; the transition from the paranoid-schizoid to the depressive position and vice-versa;[2]
symbol formation and[3] some of my previous work on the
development of verbal thought.[4] I shall not discuss them
except as factors modified by combination with each other
in a function. So much for previous work; I now give an
example of the employment of this Theory of Functions in a
psycho-analytic investigation of the field covered by the
work referred to in this chapter.

CHAPTER THREE

1. AN EMOTIONAL EXPERIENCE occurring in sleep, which I choose for reasons that will presently appear, does not differ from the emotional experience occurring during waking life in that the perceptions of the emotional experience have in both instances to be worked upon by alpha-function before they can be used for dream thoughts.

2. Alpha-function operates on the sense impressions, whatever they are, and the emotions, whatever they are, of which the patient is aware. In so far as alpha-function is successful alpha elements are produced and these elements are suited to storage and the requirements of dream thoughts. If alpha-function is disturbed, and therefore inoperative, the sense impressions of which the patient is aware and the emotions which he is experiencing remain unchanged. I shall call them beta-elements. In contrast with the alpha-elements the beta-elements are not felt to be phenomena,[1] but things in themselves.[2] The emotions likewise are objects of sense. We are thus presented with a state of mind precisely contrasting with that of the scientist who knows he is concerned with phenomena but has not the same certitude that the phenomena have a counterpart of things in themselves.

3. Beta-elements are not amenable to use in dream thoughts but are suited for use in projective identification. They are influential in producing acting out. They are objects that can be evacuated or used for a kind of thinking that depends on manipulation of what are felt to be things in themselves as if to substitute such manipulation for words or ideas. For example a man may murder his parents and so feel free to love because the anti-sexual internal parents are supposed by this act to have been evacuated. Such an act is intended

"to rid the psyche of accretions of stimuli". Beta-elements are stored but differ from alpha-elements in that they are not so much memories as undigested facts, whereas the alpha-elements have been digested by alpha-function and thus made available for thought. It is important to distinguish between memories and undigested facts—beta-elements. (The use of the terms "digested" and "undigested" will be investigated later.)

4. If the patient cannot transform his emotional experience into alpha-elements, he cannot dream. Alpha-function transforms sense impressions into alpha-elements which resemble, and may in fact be identical with, the visual images with which we are familiar in dreams, namely, the elements that Freud regards as yielding their latent content when the analyst has interpreted them. Freud showed that one of the functions of a dream is to preserve sleep. Failure of alpha-function means the patient cannot dream and therefore cannot sleep. As alpha-function makes the sense impressions of the emotional experience available for conscious and dream-thought the patient who cannot dream cannot go to sleep and cannot wake up. Hence the peculiar condition seen clinically when the psychotic patient behaves as if he were in precisely this state.

CHAPTER FOUR

1. THE EMOTIONAL EXPERIENCE must now be considered generally and not only as it occurs in sleep. I shall emphasize what I have said so far by re-writing a popular theory of the nightmare. It used once to be said that a man had a nightmare because he had indigestion and that is why he woke up in a panic. My version is: The sleeping patient is panicked; because he cannot have a nightmare he cannot wake up or go to sleep; he has had mental indigestion ever since.

2. The more general statement of the theory is this: To learn from experience alpha-function must operate on the awareness of the emotional experience; alpha-elements are produced from the impressions of the experience; these are thus made storeable and available for dream thoughts and for unconscious waking thinking. A child having the emotional experience called learning to walk is able by virtue of alpha-function to store this experience. Thoughts that had originally to be conscious become unconscious and so the child can do all the thinking needed for walking without any longer being conscious of any of it. Alpha-function is needed for conscious thinking and reasoning and for the relegation of thinking to the unconscious when it is necessary to disencumber consciousness of the burden of thought by learning a skill.

3. If there are only beta-elements, which cannot be made unconscious, there can be no repression, suppression, or learning. This creates the impression that the patient is incapable of discrimination. He cannot be unaware of any single sensory stimulus: yet such hypersensitivity is not contact with reality.

8

4. Attacks on alpha-function, stimulated by hate or envy, destroy the possibility of the patient's conscious contact either with himself or another as live objects. Accordingly we hear of inanimate objects, and even of places, when we would normally expect to hear of people. These, though described verbally, are felt by the patient to be present materially and not merely to be represented by their names. This state contrasts with animism in that live objects are endowed with the qualities of death.

CHAPTER FIVE

1. WE MUST NOW EXAMINE enforced splitting associated with a disturbed relationship with the breast or its substitutes. The infant receives milk and other creature comforts from the breast; also love, understanding, solace. Suppose his initiative is obstructed by fear of aggression, his own or another's. If the emotion is strong enough it inhibits the infant's impulse to obtain sustenance.

Love in infant or mother or both increases rather than decreases the obstruction partly because love is inseparable from envy[1] of the object so loved, partly because it is felt to arouse envy and jealousy in a third object that is excluded. The part played by love may escape notice because envy, rivalry and hate obscure it, although hate would not exist if love were not present. Violence of emotion compels reinforcement of the obstruction because violence is not distinguished from destructiveness and subsequent guilt and depression. Fear of death through starvation of essentials compels resumption of sucking. A split between material and psychical satisfaction develops.

2. Fear, hate and envy are so feared that steps are taken to destroy awareness of all feelings, although that is indistinguishable from taking life itself.[1] If a sense of reality, too great to be swamped by emotions, forces the infant to resume feeding, intolerance of envy and hate in a situation which stimulates love and gratitude leads to a splitting that differs from splitting carried out to prevent depression. It differs from splitting impelled by sadistic impulses in that its object and effect is to enable the infant to obtain what later in life would be called material comforts without acknowledging the existence of a live object on which these benefits depend.

Envy aroused by a breast that provides love, understanding, experience and wisdom, poses a problem that is solved by destruction of alpha-function. This makes breast and infant appear inanimate with consequent guiltiness, fear of suicide and fear of murder, past, present and impending. The need for love, understanding and mental development is now deflected, since it cannot be satisfied, into the search for material comforts. Since the desires for material comforts are reinforced the craving for love remains unsatisfied and turns into overweening and misdirected greed.

3. This split, enforced by starvation and fear of death through starvation on the one hand, and by love and the fear of associated murderous envy and hate on the other, produces a mental state in which the patient greedily pursues every form of material comfort; he is at once insatiable and implacable in his pursuit of satiation. Since this state originates in a need to be rid of the emotional complications of awareness of life, and a relationship with live objects, the patient appears to be incapable of gratitude or concern either for himself or others. This state involves destruction of his concern for truth. Since these mechanisms fail to rid the patient of his pains, which he feels to be due to lack of something, his pursuit of a cure takes the form of a search for a lost object and ends in increased dependence on material comfort; quantity must be the governing consideration, not quality. He feels surrounded by bizarre objects,[1] so that even the material comforts are bad and unable to satisfy his needs. But he lacks the apparatus, alpha-function, by which he might understand his predicament. The patient greedily and fearfully takes one beta-element after another apparently unable to conceive of any activity other than introjection of more beta-elements. To observe this taking place in analysis is to feel that the patient will never abandon his pursuit of a course of action which one would think he could not possibly fail to know was futile. He thinks the interpretations are without exception bad, yet he must have more and more of them. The patient however does not feel he is having interpretations for that would involve an ability to establish with the analyst the counterpart of an infant's

relationship with a breast that provides material wisdom and love. But he feels able only to establish the counterpart of a relationship in which such sustenance can be had as inanimate objects can provide; he can have analytic interpretations that he feels to be either flatus or contributions remarkable for what they are not rather than for what they are. The fact that the patient uses an equipment suited for contact with the inanimate to establish contact with himself helps to explain the confusion produced by the patient's awareness that he is in fact alive.[2] Although he feels there are no redeeming features in his environment, including in his environment the analyst's interpretations and his own lack of equipment to learn anything from his experience, the patient does ultimately grasp some of the meaning of what is said to him.

CHAPTER SIX

1. THE PATIENT'S REACTIONS to material comfort are shown by his reactions to the material comforts, the couch or other amenities, of the consulting room. Why must he have more and more of such "comforts"? Part of the answer lies in the splitting that was intended, by effecting a separation of material from psychical comforts, as an escape from fear of envy, either his own or another's.

2. The attempt to evade the experience of contact with live objects by destroying alpha-function leaves the personality unable to have a relationship with any aspect of itself that does not resemble an automaton. Only beta-elements are available for whatever activity takes the place of thinking and beta-elements are suitable for evacuation only—perhaps through the agency of projective identification. These beta-elements are dealt with by an evacuatory procedure similar to the movements of musculature, changes of mien, etc. which Freud described as intended to disencumber the personality of accretions of stimuli and not to effect changes in the environment; a muscular movement, for example, a smile, must have a different interpretation from the smile of the non-psychotic personality. The phenomena present in analysis are not identical with Freud's description of the personality acting, during the phase of dominance of the pleasure principle, to disencumber itself of accretions of stimuli. That personality is, within limits, normal; the personality I am describing is highly abnormal. Activity taking place, under the dominance of the pleasure principle, to disencumber the personality of accretions of stimuli becomes replaced, in the phase of dominance by the reality principle, by ejection of unwanted beta-elements. A smile or a verbal statement must be

interpreted as an evacuatory muscular movement and not as a communication of feeling.

The scientist whose investigations include the stuff of life itself finds himself in a situation that has a parallel in that of the patients I am describing. The breakdown in the patient's equipment for thinking leads to dominance by a mental life in which his universe is populated by inanimate objects. The inability of even the most advanced human beings to make use of their thoughts, because the capacity to think is rudimentary in all of us, means that the field for investigation, all investigation being ultimately scientific, is limited, by human inadequacy, to those phenomena that have the characteristics of the inanimate. We assume that the psychotic limitation is due to an illness: but that that of the scientist is not. Investigation of the assumption illuminates disease on the one hand and scientific method on the other. It appears that our rudimentary equipment for "thinking" thoughts is adequate when the problems are associated with the inanimate, but not when the object for investigation is the phenomenon of life itself. Confronted with the complexities of the human mind the analyst must be circumspect in following even accepted scientific method; its weakness may be closer to the weakness of psychotic thinking than superficial scrutiny would admit.

CHAPTER SEVEN

1. IF A MAN has an emotional experience when asleep or awake and is able to convert it into alpha-elements he can either remain unconscious of that emotional experience or become conscious of it. The sleeping man has an emotional experience, converts it into alpha-elements and so becomes capable of dream thoughts. Thus he is free to become conscious (that is wake up) and describe the emotional experience by a narrative usually known as a dream.

2. A man talking to a friend converts the sense impressions of this emotional experience into alpha-elements, thus becoming capable of dream thoughts and therefore of undisturbed consciousness of the facts whether the facts are the events in which he participates or his feelings about those events or both. He is able to remain "asleep" or unconscious of certain elements that cannot penetrate the barrier presented by his "dream". Thanks to the "dream" he can continue uninterruptedly to be awake, that is, awake to the fact that he is talking to his friend, but asleep to elements which, if they could penetrate the barrier of his "dreams", would lead to domination of his mind by what are ordinarily unconscious ideas and emotions.

The dream makes a barrier against mental phenomena which might overwhelm the patient's awareness that he is talking to a friend, and, at the same time, makes it impossible for awareness that he is talking to a friend to overwhelm his phantasies. The psychotic's attempt to discriminate one from the other leads to rational thought characterized by a peculiar lack of "resonance". What he says clearly and in articulated speech is one dimensional. It has no overtones or undertones of meaning. It makes the listener inclined to say "so what?" It has no capacity to evoke a train of thought.

3. The "dream" has many of the functions of censorship and resistance. These functions are not the product of the unconscious but instruments by which the "dream" creates and differentiates consciousness from unconsciousness.

To sum up: the "dream", together with the alpha-function, which makes dream possible, is central to the operation of consciousness and unconsciousness, on which ordered thought depends. Alpha-function theory of the "dream" has the elements of the view represented by classical psycho-analytic dream theory, that is to say, censorship and resistance are represented in it. But in alpha-function theory the powers of censorship and resistance are essential to differentiation of conscious and unconscious and help to maintain the discrimination between the two. This discrimination derives from the operation of the "dream", which is a combination in narrative form of dream thoughts, which thoughts in turn derive from combinations of alpha-elements. In this theory the ability to "dream" preserves the personality from what is virtually a psychotic state. It therefore helps to explain the tenacity with which the dream, as represented in classical theory, defends itself against the attempt to make the unconscious conscious. Such an attempt must appear indistinguishable from destruction of the capacity to dream in so far as that capacity is related to differentiating conscious from unconscious[1] and maintaining the difference so established.

CHAPTER EIGHT

1. I SHALL NOW TRANSFER all that I have said about the establishment of conscious and unconscious and a barrier between them to a supposed entity, that I designate a "contact-barrier"; Freud used this term to describe the neuro-physiological entity subsequently known as a synapse. In conformity with this my statement that the man has to "dream" a current emotional experience whether it occurs in sleep or in waking life is re-formulated thus: The man's alpha-function whether in sleeping or waking transforms the sense-impressions related to an emotional experience, into alpha-elements, which cohere as they proliferate to form the contact-barrier. This contact-barrier, thus continuously in process of formation, marks the point of contact and separation between conscious and unconscious elements and originates the distinction between them. The nature of the contact-barrier will depend on the nature of the supply of alpha-elements and on the manner of their relationship to each other. They may cohere. They may be agglomerated. They may be ordered sequentially to give the appearance of narrative (at least in the form in which the contact-barrier may reveal itself in a dream). They may be ordered logically. They may be ordered geometrically.

2. The term "contact-barrier" emphasizes the establishment of contact between conscious and unconscious and the selective passage of elements from one to the other. On the nature of the contact-barrier will depend the change of elements from conscious to unconscious and vice versa. In so far as dreams give us direct access to its study they retain the central position in psycho-analysis that Freud assigned to them.

The nature of the transition from conscious to unconscious and vice versa, and therefore the nature of the contact-barrier and its component alpha-elements affect memory and the characteristics of any given memory.

3. In practice the theory of functions and the theory of an alpha-function make possible interpretations showing precisely how the patient feels that he has feelings, but cannot learn from them; sensations, some of which are extremely faint, but cannot learn from them either. A determination not to experience anything can be shown to co-exist with an inability to reject or ignore any stimulus. Sense-impressions can be seen to have some meaning but the patient feels incapable of knowing what the meaning is.

4. Interpretations derived from these theories appear to effect changes in the patient's capacity for thinking and therefore of understanding. Such a response is itself sufficiently peculiar, in view of the phenomenon being investigated, to require explanation. In the first place the nature of the difficulties, if indeed they are being accurately described, would seem to rule out the possibility that the patient could grasp the description. Such a difficulty may be surmounted by an elucidation of different degrees of disability. From the point of view of technique it would be agreeable if the response to interpretations based on a use of a theory of functions, alpha-function and contact-barrier carried some element of confirmation that a realization approximated to these theoretical concepts. Scientifically, validation of the theory would then be supported by a correlation between evidence that capacity for thinking had been increased by analysis and evidence of the existence of a realization that corresponded to the abstract theoretical construct. There is in fact an "echo" effect when an interpretation is given that lends support to the idea that the theoretical concept of contact-barrier has a corresponding realization. Discussion of this is outside the scope of this subject and I leave it for another occasion.

In Chapters 3–8 I have used the concept of alpha-function to fill gaps in my knowledge of a state of mind which is met with in analytic practice and that I want to describe. I have thus been able to proceed with the communication without having to wait for discovery of the missing facts and without making statements that might appear to suggest that the facts were already known.

I must now show how the theory of functions is used as a tool in the analytic work. I give examples of the background of emotional experiences (realizations) from which the theory was abstracted and pass on to give examples of realizations, unknown when the theory was abstracted, that were subsequently found to approximate to the theory. The material unfortunately does not lend itself to such logical exposition without producing misleading distortion of the facts. In the next chapter emphasis is on the background of emotional experience from which the theory is abstracted. The description is of elements from which the abstraction was made but these are mixed with so many others that it is impossible to claim for it qualities that are ordinarily regarded as essential to a scientific production.

CHAPTER NINE

1. A SMALL NUMBER of patients with whom I have had to deal have presented prominently symptoms of disordered capacity for thought. In the course of their treatment opportunities for orthodox transference interpretations occurred and were taken, but the patient often learned nothing from them. The stream of disjointed associations continued. Interpretations based on theories of anal erotism in its various forms, theories of the patient's need to improvise a personality out of elements he felt were worthless and which he could therefore afford to lose, theories of splitting, projective identification, defence against assault and so on had only slight effect. There were signs of confusion that I had learned to associate with projective identification. I therefore assumed that I was the repository of a part of his personality such as his sanity, or the non-psychotic part of his personality. Before long I decided that further interpretations based on these theories were not likely to achieve any useful purpose. I tested the supposition that I contained the non-psychotic part of his personality, and then began to be aware that I was supposed to be conscious of what was going on while he was not. I was (contained) his "conscious". Sometimes I could visualize the situation, unfolding in the analysis, as one in which the patient was a fœtus to whom the mother's emotions were communicated but to whom the stimulus for the emotions, and their source, was unknown (see "model making", p. 66 below). At other times he seemed to have a rudimentary idea of what was going on, but no idea how he felt. I shall not here describe the variations on this theme, as they were not substantially different from those described by M. Klein, H. Rosenfeld and others. The problem which awaited

solution, and which I am now discussing, was to determine
what this part was. The theory of functions offered a pros-
pect of solving this problem by assuming that I contained unknown functions of his personality and from this to scrutinize
the sessional experience for clues of what these might be. I
assumed that I was "consciousness." Freud's theory that
consciousness is the sense-organ of psychic quality, allowed
an assumption that a separation was being effected between
consciousness and psychic quality. This assumption proved
fruitful, but only for a session or two and then I found myself
in the same situation as before, or nearly so. I was still
thinking of the problem as one that could be solved in terms
of transference theory and projective identification, that is to
say, that I could assume that patients felt under scrutiny by
me and the parts of their personality I was supposed to contain. In the light of theories of transference and projective
identifications the material poured out could be seen as the
link between patient and analyst and I could interpret in
the way described in Attacks on Linking. Interpretations
had some success, but I did not feel that changes necessarily
related to illumination received from interpretations. It
then occurred to me that he was doing what I earlier described as "dreaming" the immediate events in the analysis—
that is to say, translating sense impressions into alpha-
elements. This idea seemed to illuminate sometimes but
became dynamic only when I related it to *defective* alpha-
function, that is to say, when it occurred to me that I was
witnessing an inability to dream through lack of alpha-
elements and therefore an inability to sleep or wake, to be
either conscious or unconscious.

2. This could explain why I was a conscious that was
incapable of the functions of consciousness and he an
"unconscious" incapable of the functions of *unconsciousness*.
(For the sake of simplicity I am supposing that this division
of functions remained stationary, but in fact it was not so;
roles were interchangeable.)

3. Now this situation does not correspond to the theoretical
framework I have suggested, the theory, namely, of a
contact-barrier owing its existence to the proliferation of

alpha-elements by alpha-function and serving the function of a membrane which by the nature of its composition and permeability separates mental phenomena into two groups one of which performs the functions of consciousness and the other the functions of unconsciousness.

4. In the new situation there is a division of sorts, suspended between analyst and patient as it were, but offering no resistance to the passage of elements from the one zone to the other. It is unsuited to the establishment of conscious and unconscious, and therefore conducive to defective or anomalous developments of a capacity for memory and repression. The difference in the two states derives from the differences between a contact-barrier composed of alpha-elements and one composed, if that is the right word, of beta-elements. These last, it will be remembered, appear to lack a capacity for linkage with each other. Clinically this screen of beta-elements presents itself to casual observation as indistinguishable from a confused state and in particular from any one of that class of confused states which resemble dreams, namely: 1. An outpouring of disjointed phrases and images which, if the patient were asleep, we would certainly believe to be evidence that the patient was dreaming. 2. A similar outpouring but expressed in a manner that suggests that the patient is feigning dream. 3. A confused outpouring that seems to be evidence of hallucination. 4. Similar to (3) but suggestive of an hallucination of a dream; I have not had occasion to suppose that the patient was having a dream that he was hallucinated. All four states are related to a fear lest the depressive position should precipitate a murderous superego and therefore to the need to have the emotional experience in which this might occur in the presence of the analyst. Clinically the screen of beta-elements to which I am referring bears a strong superficial resemblance to any one of these four classes and might be supposed to be identical with them.

5. Comparison of the beta-element screen with the confused states resembling dream shows the beta-element screen to be coherent and purposive. An interpretation that the patient was pouring out a stream of material intended to

destroy the analyst's psycho-analytic potency would not seem out of place. Equally apt would be an interpretation that the patient was concerned to withhold rather than to impart information. One peculiarity of the situation is the plethora of interpretations that would occur to anyone with any common sense. Yet they do not occur to the patient. These common-sense interpretations have a common characteristic in that all are accusatory, or, alternatively, laudatory as if far-fetched with intent to reassure the patient of his goodness in the teeth of the evidence. This is not fortuitous; it would be difficult in face of the evidence to maintain that it was. One is forced to a conclusion that is unexpected and surprising, namely, that the beta-element screen—I shall call it beta-screen for short in future—has a quality enabling it to evoke the kind of response the patient desires, or, alternatively, a response from the analyst which is heavily charged with counter-transference. Both possibilities require examination for their implications.

CHAPTER TEN

1. THANKS TO THE BETA-SCREEN the psychotic patient has a capacity for evoking emotions in the analyst; his associations are the elements of the beta-screen intended to evoke interpretations or other responses which are less related to his need for psycho-analytic interpretation than to his need to produce an emotional involvement.[1] The theory of counter transferences offers only partly satisfactory explanation because it is concerned with the manifestation as a symptom of the analyst's unconscious motives and therefore leaves the patient's contribution unexplained. First the patient for which these theories are intended is not employing articulate speech; he is demonstrating with evident sincerity an inability to understand his own state of mind even when it is pointed out to him. His use of words is much closer to action intended to "unburden the psyche of accretions of stimuli" than to speech. Second, he does not set to work to manipulate the analyst in the same way as the neurotic. There is a consistency in the characteristics of beta-elements. The language I must use to describe a dynamic situation produces a distortion because it is the language of a scientific method designed for the study of the inanimate. This distortion affects my claim that certain characteristics of the beta-screen are consistent. It would be more true to say that a dynamic situation evolves and that its evolution is betrayed by the emergence of a particular characteristic as one that pervades a growing number of elements and gives them consistency. The replacement of a contact-barrier by a beta-screen is a living process. The observations of the analyst, for reasons connected with the nature of the change from paranoid-schizoid to depressive position and vice versa,

contributes to the analytic situation an element which makes its development appear to be a transition from a series of discrete particles or elements to a synthesis of these same elements. One replaces the other in a manner analogous to the replacement of one judgment by another when we examine a figure illustrating reversible perspective.

2. The analysand contributes changes which are associated with the replacement of alpha-function by what may be described as a reversal of direction of the function.[1] Instead of sense impressions being changed into alpha-elements for use in dream thoughts and unconscious waking thinking, the development of the contact-barrier is replaced by its destruction. This is effected by the reversal of alpha-function so that the contact-barrier and the dream thoughts and unconscious waking thinking which are the texture of the contact-barrier are turned into alpha-elements, divested[2] of all characteristics that separate them from beta-elements and are then projected thus forming the beta-screen.

3. Reversal of alpha-function means the dispersal of the contact-barrier and is quite compatible with the establishment of objects with the characteristics I once ascribed to bizarre objects. The compatability would be much increased if, despite my warning that contact-barrier (a function) and ego (a structure) should not be regarded as interchangeable terms referring to the same thing, we could consider that the reversal of alpha-function did in fact affect the ego and therefore did not produce a simple return to beta-elements, but objects which differ in important respects from the original beta-elements which had no tincture of the personality adhering to them. The beta-element differs from the bizarre object in that the bizarre object is beta-element plus ego and superego traces. The reversal of alpha-function does violence to the structure associated with alpha-function.

4. To review the terms I have used so far: (1) the ego is a structure that, as Freud describes it, is a specialized development from the id having the function of establishing contact between psychic and external reality. (2) Alpha-function is the name given to an abstraction used by the analyst to

describe a function, of which he does not know the nature, until such time he feels in position to replace it by factors for which he feels he has obtained evidence in the course of the investigation in which he is employing alpha-function. It corresponds to that function of a number of factors, including the function of the ego, that transforms sense data into alpha-elements. Alpha-elements comprise visual images, auditory patterns, olfactory patterns, and are suitable for employment in dream thoughts, unconscious waking thinking, dreams, contact-barrier, memory. Clinically the bizarre object which is suffused with superego characteristics comes nearest to providing a realization to correspond with the concept of beta-elements. But the concept of beta-element includes only sense-impressions, the sense-impression as if it were a part of the personality experiencing the sense impression, and the sense-impression as if it were the thing-in-itself to which the sense-impression corresponds.

It is to be noted that the alpha-function may be regarded as a structure, a piece of mental apparatus producing the contact-barrier. In turn the contact-barrier may be regarded, as the name I have given it suggests, as having the characteristics of a structure. This is a repetition of the problem implicit in the differentiation from each other of ego, consciousness and alpha-function, and it is worth considering the implications of this peculiarity of psycho-analytic investigation, namely the use of concepts relating to objects which we need sometimes to consider as if they were related to machines, that is to say as if they were inanimate, and sometimes as if they were functions, which, since we are dealing with human beings and not machines, are certain to be suffused with the characteristics of life. In the case of alpha-function used as an unknown to correspond with a realization which is changing from unknown to known the name given these objects should make it clear whether we are to observe the object in its character as a function or as a structure or as an abstraction.

The contact-barrier may be expected to manifest itself clinically—if indeed it is manifest at all—as something that resembles dreams. As we have seen the contact-barrier permits a relationship and preservation of belief in it as an event in actuality, subject to the laws of nature, without having that view submerged by emotions and phantasies originating endo-psychically. Reciprocally it preserves emotions with endo-psychic origin from being overwhelmed by the realistic view. The contact-barrier is therefore responsible for the preservation of the distinction between conscious and unconscious and for its inception. The unconscious is thus preserved. It is being recruited by alpha-function with alpha-elements that need to be stored, but inhibited from intrusion into consciousness on occasions when their impingement on the man's grasp of the situation of external reality would be felt as an irrelevance or a dislocation of ordered thought.

CHAPTER ELEVEN

1. THE THEORY OF FUNCTIONS and the theory of alpha-function in particular makes possible further contributions to an understanding of thought processes. I shall consider the nature and function of thinking in any situation that seems to mirror an early age in the life of man, or his current primitive depths, where it would be possible to detect the qualities we associate with thought. In his paper on Two Principles of Mental Functioning Freud says "Restraint of motor discharge (of action) had now become necessary and was provided by means of the process of *thought*, which was developed from ideation. Thought was endowed with qualities which made it possible for the mental apparatus to support increased tension during a delay in the process of discharge. It is essentially an experimental way of acting, accompanied by displacement of smaller quantities of cathexis together with less expenditure (discharge) of them." He continues "For this purpose conversion of free cathexis into 'bound' cathexis was imperative, and this was brought about by means of raising the level of the whole cathectic process." He continues "It is probable that thinking was originally unconscious, in so far as it rose above mere ideation and turned to the relations between the object-impressions, and that it became endowed with further qualities which were perceptible to consciousness only through its connection with the memory traces of words." Implicit in Freud's statement is the part played by intolerance of frustration in producing tension, and then its relief, by the employment of thought to fill the interval between the need to unburden the psyche of accretions of stimuli and the actual unburdening. The

link between intolerance of frustration and the development of thought is central to an understanding of thought
and its disturbances. Freud's statement suggests that the
reality principle is sequent to the pleasure principle; it needs
modification to make both principles co-exist. Though I
shall not immediately discuss it I make a reservation that intolerance of frustration may be excessive, a quantitative change
which almost becomes one of kind. Let us now suppose intolerance of frustration allied to hunger: suppose further that
satisfaction of hunger is made impossible by other factors in
the personality such as fear, greed, or envy that cannot allow
the breast or its equivalent any success in satisfying the
envious person. In such a situation greed would be intensified
and so would the intolerance of frustration; the effect
would be much the same as if the personality were endowed
with an excessive intolerance of frustration. Does it matter
if intolerance of frustration, or any other dynamic characteristic is primary or secondary? The distinction indicates the
limitation of any treatment effecting changes in the personality to secondary factors for primary factors will not be
altered.

It is likely from clinical evidence of the infant's need for
material and psychological support that no distinction between material and psychological can be made by the infant.
In analysis, however, it is possible to deduce whether the
deficiency was one of physical or psychical quality. No
matter how early such a deficiency might be, nor what it
might be due to, it would be felt to be real and would demand
a real solution, that is, one that appeared to remove the
disease. The choice that matters to the psycho-analyst is one
that lies between *procedures designed to evade frustration and
those designed to modify it. That is the critical decision.*

There are other ways in which the procedure adopted may
be classified, as, for example, those that are ultimately
destined to reveal themselves as belonging to the class of
muscular action (physical movement generally) and those
that are destined to develop so that they are ultimately
classified as pertaining to the realms of thought. The fact
that the decision is related to such an ultimate classification

is significant but for the present I wish to focus attention on phenomena genetically related to the co-existence in the personality of feelings of frustration, intolerance of feelings of frustration, related emotions and the decision that emerges from such a concatenation of elements.

CHAPTER TWELVE

1. THE ACTIVITY WE KNOW as "thinking" was in origin a procedure for unburdening the psyche of accretions of stimuli and the mechanism is that which has been described by Melanie Klein as projective identification. The broad outline of this theory is that there exists an omnipotent phantasy that it is possible to split off temporarily undesired, though sometimes valued, parts of the personality and put them into an object. In practice it is possible, and desirable in the interests of beneficial therapy, to observe and interpret the evidence that supports this theory and which this theory explains in a way that no other theory does.

2. It is also possible, and in fact essential, to observe evidence which shows that a patient in whom the operation of this omnipotent phantasy can be deduced is capable of behaviour which is related to a counterpart in reality of this phantasy. The patient, even at the outset of life, has contact with reality sufficient to enable him to act in a way that engenders in the mother feelings that he does not want, or which he wants the mother to have. To make theory correspond to these clinical findings I have suggested an emended version of Freud's pleasure principle theory so that the reality principle should be considered to operate co-existentially with the pleasure principle. An instance of an attempt to make the omnipotent phantasy a reality can be seen in the patient who has the impulse to force others to feel that he is capable of murdering the sexual parents so that he may feel capable of a loving sexual relationship free from the fear that he would murder his partner and himself if, as he would be bound to do, he observed himself and his partner displaying evidence of mutual sexual passion. I have suggested

that in an extreme form this may even lead to murder as a method of giving effect, in the world of reality, to the omnipotent phantasy of projective identification which, without such action, would remain only an omnipotent phantasy.

3. There are instances far less dramatic and therefore demanding some perspicacity in the analyst to discern them. It is of importance that the analyst should observe them. That is to say, he should observe and interpret the operation of the phantasy as a mental phenomenon deducible from the evidence and also observe signs that the patient is sufficiently adjusted to reality to be able to manipulate his environment so that the phantasy of projective identification appears to have substance in reality.

4. The more this realistic component is in evidence, and can be made evident to the patient, the more it is possible to judge the extent to which a gravely ill and indeed certifiable patient has contact with reality albeit a reality not always familiar to better developed individuals.

5. The patient's ability to gear his omnipotent phantasy of projective identification to reality is directly related to his capacity for tolerance of frustration. If he cannot tolerate frustration the omnipotent phantasy of projective identification has proportionately less factual counterpart in external reality. This contributes to the state Melanie Klein describes as *excessive* projective identification. The excess however must be scrutinized carefully. It may appear to be excessive because the analyst is forced to be aware of it by the realistic steps which the patient takes to make the analyst in fact experience emotions of a kind the patient does not want to have (M. Klein). *This* excess must be sharply distinguished from the excessive projective identification which represents a resort to omnipotent phantasy as a flight from reality, and in particular from feelings which are not wanted. But projective identification cannot exist without its reciprocal, namely an introjective activity intended to lead to an accumulation of good internal objects.

6. Let us now suppose that in reality the breast supplies the infant with milk and sensations of security, warmth,

well-being, love. Let us suppose further that the infant needs —I deliberately avoid saying "wishes"—to possess itself of the milk itself and the related sensations. We may make a distinction between milk and love by appropriate classification or we may emphasize, if it suits us, the respects in which they appear similar. Thus we may say that milk is a material substance and is related to alimentation and is presumably dealt with by the digestive tract. Love on the other hand we may regard as immaterial though comparable with milk for the mental welfare[1] of the child. We may place it in one or more of a number of different categories that philosophy, religion and other disciplines place at our disposal. The only reason for limiting our classificatory apparatus to one discipline is the desire to achieve simplicity. Whether we employ philosophical concepts, religious concepts, endocrinological concepts or concepts employed by the neuro-physiologist they will be open to the same objection, namely that they describe states of mind with which we are familiar and shall require them to describe phenomena, or the realities we assume to be the counterpart of those phenomena, with which we are not familar but believe we have correctly observed and correctly imputed to the infant. Two adults may mean widely different things by the same word "love", yet this word is one I must use to describe part of what I believe to be an infant's experience (I include lack of love). It is clear therefore that there are two major sources of error that immediately present themselves, one being the semantic gap which has to be bridged between adults discussing the problem and the other the scientific propriety of attributing to infant experience a modified yet recognizably similar experience.

7. The milk, we may assume with a degree of conviction we cannot feel about love, is received and dealt with by the alimentary canal; what receives and deals with the love? The question may be a formulation based on inadequate thinking, and therefore liable to lead to error, unless we consider what the situation is with the mother. As the infant receives the milk and deals with it by the alimentary system, so the mother provides it by the glandular system, yet milk has been known to fail and the failure has been attributed to emotional upsets.

The infant likewise has been supposed to suffer digestive disturbances originating in an emotional upset. It may be useful to suppose that there exists in reality a psycho-somatic breast and an infantile psycho-somatic alimentary canal corresponding to the breast.[1] This breast is an object the infant needs to supply it with milk and good internal objects. I do not attribute to the infant an awareness of this need; but I do attribute to the infant an awareness of a need not satisfied. We can say the infant feels frustrated if we assume the existence of some apparatus with which frustration can be experienced. Freud's concept of consciousness as that of "a sense-organ for the perception of psychical qualities", provides such an apparatus.

8. As the analyst treating an adult patient I can be conscious of something of which the patient is not conscious. Similarly the mother can discern a state of mind in her infant before the infant can be conscious of it, as, for example, when the baby shows signs of needing food before it is properly aware of it. In this imaginary situation the need for the breast is a feeling and that feeling itself is a bad breast; the infant does not feel it wants a good breast but it does feel it wants to evacuate a bad one.

9. Suppose the infant is fed; the taking in of milk, warmth, love, may be felt as taking in a good breast. Under dominance of the, at first unopposed, bad breast, "taking in" food may be felt as indistinguishable from evacuating a bad breast. Both good and bad breasts are felt as possessing the same degree of concreteness and reality as milk. Sooner or later the "wanted" breast is felt as an "idea of a breast missing" and not as a bad breast present. We can see that the bad, that is to say wanted but absent, breast is much more likely to become recognized as an idea than the good breast which is associated with what a philosopher would call a thing-in-itself or a thing-in-actuality, in that the sense of a good breast depends on the existence of milk the infant has in fact taken. The good breast and the bad breast, the one being associated with the actual milk that satisfies hunger and the other with the non-existence of that milk, must have a difference in psychical quality. "Thoughts are

a nuisance" said one of my patients, "I don't want them."
Is a "thought" the same as an absence of a thing? If there
is no "thing", is "no thing" a thought and is it by virtue of
the fact that there is "no thing" that one recognizes that
"it" must be thought? Before considering further how this
difference in quality might be establ:shed I shall assume
another situation. Let us suppose the infant to have fed but
to be feeling unloved. Again it is aware of a need for the
good breast and again this "need for a good breast" is a
"bad breast" that needs to be evacuated. A number of
different situations of this kind would pose problems re-
quiring different solutions; in my first example the infant
could be supposed to feel that the "need for the breast" bad
breast was being evacuated if it passed a motion while taking
milk; in that case it would associate a physical act with a
result that we would call a change in its state of mind from
dissatisfaction to satisfaction. If it is correct to suppose that
the central question rests on discrimination of psychical
quality and if consciousness is legitimately regarded as the
sense-organ of psychical quality it is difficult to see how
consciousness comes into existence. It clearly will not do to say
that the infant is conscious of psychical quality and transforms
this emotional experience into alpha-elements for I have
already said the existence of consciousness and unconsciousness depends on the prior production of alpha-elements by
alpha-function. We must assume that the good breast and
the bad breast are emotional experiences. The physical
component, milk, discomfort of satiation or the opposite,
can be immediately apparent to the sense and we can therefore accord a chronological priority to beta-elements over
alpha-elements. Intolerance of frustration could be so pro-
nounced that alpha-function would be forestalled by immediate evacuation of the beta-elements. The mental component, love, security, anxiety, as distinct from the somatic
requires a process analogous to digestion. What this might
be is concealed by use of the concept of alpha-function but
a value may be found for this by psycho-analytic investigations. For example, when the mother loves the infant what
does she do it with? Leaving aside the physical channels of

communication my impression is that her love is expressed
by reverie.

10. Though the difficulties of penetrating the adult mind
in analysis are great they are less so than attempting to
penetrate the infant's by speculative hypothesis; investigation of reverie in the adult may afford us an entry into this
problem. We may deduce from reverie, as the psychological
source of supply of the infant's needs for love and understanding, what kind of psychological receptor organ is required if the infant is to be able to profit from reverie as it is
able, thanks to the digestive capacities of the alimentary
canal, to profit from the breast and the milk it supplies.
Put in another way, assuming alpha-function as that which
makes available to the infant what would otherwise remain
unavailable for any purpose other than evacuation as beta-
elements, what are the *factors* of this function that relate
directly to the mother's capacity for reverie?

11. The mother's capacity for reverie is here considered
as inseparable from the content for clearly one depends on the
other. If the feeding mother cannot allow reverie or if the
reverie is allowed but is not associated with love for the child
or its father this fact will be communicated to the infant
even though incomprehensible to the infant. Psychical
quality will be imparted to the channels of communication,
the links with the child. What happens will depend on the
nature of these maternal psychical qualities and their impact
on the psychical qualities of the infant, for the impact of the
one upon the other is an emotional experience subject, from
the point of view of the development of the couple and the
individuals composing it, to transformation by alpha-function.
The term reverie may be applied to almost any content. I
wish to reserve it only for such content as is suffused with
love or hate. Using it in this restricted sense reverie is that
state of mind which is open to the reception of any "objects"
from the loved object and is therefore capable of reception
of the infant's projective identifications whether they are
felt by the infant to be good or bad. In short, reverie is a
factor of the mother's alpha-function.

12. Returning now to the infant containing[1] a "need for

the breast" which I have said is a feeling that is equated with a "bad breast".[2] This bad breast has to be exchanged for a good breast. An infant capable of tolerating frustration can permit itself to have a sense of reality, to be dominated by the reality principle. If its intolerance of frustration reaches beyond a certain degree omnipotent mechanisms come into operation, notably projective identification. This might still be regarded as realistic, in that it suggests awareness of the value of a capacity for thought as a means of softening frustration when the reality principle is dominant. But it depends for its efficacy on the existence of the mother's capacity for reverie. If the mother fails then a further burden is thrown on the infant's capacity for toleration of frustration for now its capacity for toleration of frustration of thought itself is tested. I am here supposing that projective identification is an early form of that which later is called a capacity for thinking. An infant endowed with marked capacity for toleration of frustration might survive the ordeal of a mother incapable of reverie and therefore incapable of supplying its mental needs. At the other extreme an infant markedly incapable of tolerating frustration cannot survive without breakdown even the experience of projective identification with a mother capable of reverie; nothing less than unceasing breast feeding would serve and that is not possible through lack of appetite if for no other reason. We have thus approached a mental life unmapped by the theories elaborated for the understanding of neurosis. I do not propose to pursue this investigation now, except in so far as it bears on alpha-function.

CHAPTER THIRTEEN

1. FOR EFFECTIVE USE it is necessary to be able to regard alpha-function as constant by virtue of its status as an unknown. In so far as it is flexible its flexibility derives from the use of variables as factors that can be replaced, as I explained earlier, by theories and concepts of fixed value. The values given to the variables (the factors) must be genuinely constant so that once their value has been fixed the meaning of alpha-function is fixed. In practice even an approximation to precision is only possible in the sense that the factor must be clearly described or, in the instance of a theory, correctly quoted.[1]

2. As an example of an attempt at precise formulation I take alpha-function and two factors, excessive projective identification and excess of bad objects. Suppose that in the course of the analysis these two factors are obtrusive to the exclusion of other factors that the analyst has observed. If psycho-analytic theory were rationally organized it should be possible to refer to both these factors by symbols which were part of a system of reference that was applied uniformly and universally. The Kleinian theory of projective identification would be referred to by initials and a page and paragraph reference. Similarly, Freud's view of attention would be replaced by a reference. This can in fact be done, though clumsily, by reference to page and line of a standard edition even now. Such a statement could lend itself to mere manipulation, more or less ingenious, of symbols according to apparently arbitrary rules. Provided that the analyst preserves a sense of the factual background to which such a formulation refers, there are advantages in the exercise in precision and rigour of thought that is exacted by an attempt to

concentrate actual clinical experience so that it may be expressed in such abstract notation. Further the analyst can see from an inspection of his formalizations which theories he is using and which he neglects. From evidence of neglect he could deduce either that his psycho-analytic armoury was becoming impoverished or that certain psycho-analytic theories were not in his experience standing up well to the test of clinical usefulness. In either case this would be a valuable insight. The formula provides a shorthand summary of sessions over a period. It should be possible to see what links one summary has with another thence to predict by reference to the theoretical deductive systems in which these factors appear as hypotheses or premises analytical situations that may develop. Alpha-function may be a major pre-occupation of the analyst in a particular analysis, but it does not follow that it will continue to be so, or that, being so, it will have the same value in subsequent weeks. In the next group of sessions it may become clear that a belief that a bad object exists is being expressed as an expression of envious disparagement of a good object. In that case the formulation will reflect the change of factors. By the next week alpha-function may no longer be of central importance and other factors and some other function may have taken its place. The principle of applying the Theory of Functions remains the same whatever the function and whatever the factors of which it is the function.

3. As a method of making something clear to himself the analyst needs his own book of psycho-analytic theories that he personally frequently uses together with page and paragraph numbers that make their identification certain.

4. The capacity to remember what the patient has said needs to be allied to a capacity for forgetting so that the fact that any session is a new session and therefore an unknown situation that must be psycho-analytically investigated is not obscured by an already over-plentiful fund of pre-and misconception. Yet the analyst needs all the knowledge of the patient and the discoveries and work of his predecessor in the field that he can muster. This reinforces the need for a firm

structure, a theoretical framework of psycho-analysis which is yet capable of flexibility in action. If the rigidity of the theoretical structure is weakened by departure from theory such departures become easier to detect. For example, if reference to transference is made by specific quotation it can be seen that the writer is claiming to use the term with meanings already established. If conscious anxiety about the analyst is said to be a factor in the transference it would be apparent that the writer had in mind some phenomenon not the same as that described by Freud in the passage to which reference is made. Flexibility is conferred by working with functions that are variables whose value only becomes constant when for the variables of which it is the function there are substituted factors which are constants. At present the nearest to a constant in psycho-analysis is the use of a page and line reference to the theory that is being employed as a factor.

5. With the deterioration in the analyst's theoretical and analytical equipment I need not concern myself here; it is sufficient that a method of formulation would help to make it manifest, and enable the analyst to take such steps as he thought necessary. Diminished use of a psycho-analytic theory might show that it was not surviving the test of analytical practice.

6. A record of sessions that showed succinctly the progress of the analysis by representing the theories employed would thus serve a purpose that was more than an aid to the analyst's memory. Its value as a record of work done, and indirectly of the analyst's method of working, would be great, but the central problem concerns the need for a system of notation that is valuable both for recording analytic problems and working on them.

7. The system of notation must make it possible for the analyst to provide a record that he himself can understand, after a lapse of time, and that can be communicated to others without serious loss of meaning. Difficult as it may be to fulfil this ambition its achievement would not be enough. For development of psycho-analysis a notation must be found that records psycho-analytic work, as mathematical notation

records facts, but just as mathematical notation records facts and provides a means for calculation as well, so the ideal psycho-analytic notation must provide a means for working on the problem that the notation has enabled the analyst to record.

CHAPTER FOURTEEN

1. A CENTRAL PART is played by alpha-function in transforming an emotional experience into alpha-elements because a sense of reality matters to the individual in the way that food, drink, air and excretion of waste products matter. Failure to eat, drink or breathe properly has disastrous consequences for life itself. Failure to use the emotional experience produces a comparable disaster in the development of the personality; I include amongst these disasters degrees of psychotic deterioration that could be described as death of the personality. As always, the use of a model, as I am using the model of the digestive system here, is open to the dangers I discuss on p. 80. To moderate these dangers and make discussion scientific a notation to represent emotional experience is required. If the individual analyst built up for himself an anthology of working psycho-analytic theory on a foundation of a few good basic theories well understood and capable, individually and in combination, of covering a great many of the situations he might expect to meet, it might help the creation of a notation. What follows is a sketch to indicate the lines along which progress could be made and which I have found helpful.

2. The feelings we know by the names "love" and "hate" would seem to be obvious choices if the criterion is basic emotion. Envy and Gratitude, Depression, Guilt, Anxiety, all occupy a dominant place in psycho-analytic theory and would seem with Sex to be choices to place with love and hate. In fact I prefer three factors I regard as intrinsic to the link between objects considered to be in relationship with each other. An emotional experience cannot be conceived of in isolation from a relationship. The basic relationships

that I postulate are (1) X loves Y; (2) X hates Y; and (3) X knows Y. These links will be expressed by the signs L, H and K. What realization may exist to which these abstract links, L, H and K, correspond? Suppose an imaginary situation of a type with which an analyst is familiar; the patient Smith is talking freely and is co-operative and friendly; in the course of his associations he mentions that he knows a certain psycho-therapist, Jones, who is a very stupid man and knows virtually nothing about psycho-analysis. The patient knows him well and has good reason, he says, to dislike him. He once treated a friend of his, Mr. May, with shocking results. His friend's marriage, which had always been harmonious until his friend took up treatment . . . . etc. Obviously this is a complex communication. There is a link between the patient and the analyst; there are various links between the patient and the psycho-therapist, between patient and his friend, between the patient and his friend's analyst. For the link between the patient and analyst there is direct evidence. With regard to the patient's report of the other links the evidence is mostly indirect although the direct evidence which the session affords could be used, if thought desirable, to supplement the patient's own statements. The patient says he knows Jones. Is this to be recorded as Smith K Jones? He says he dislikes Jones. Should it be Smith H Jones? The patient says "his friend" Mr. May. Should this then be Smith L May? Or is there some previous material in the analysis, or some manner or intonation that suggests a link, Smith L Mrs. May? But perhaps there is some material that suggests there is a homosexual relationship between Smith and Mr. May? There need be no end to the questions stimulated by an imaginary episode or limit to the number of answers for each question. But it is hardly less true to say just that about a real session. Yet on the answers to the questions, which the analyst begins to entertain, will depend his interpretation of the direct evidence of the nature of the transference. It may seem, since the analytic situation is complex, that there can be no merit in recording it by one of three simple signs. Admitting that the sign is to express only one part of the emotional experience, the link, does not the imaginary episode show that either the signs, L, H and K, conceal a complex link which may have endless varieties under a sign of misleading simplicity, or, that they define a link with a degree of rigidity which makes their applications to a real analytical situation a hopeless falsification?

3. There is no reason for either of these alternatives to be true; the signs can be related to fact in a way that saves them from becoming meaningless symbols and can at the same time be sufficiently abstract to ensure that they are generally and not merely accidentally applicable to real emotional situations.

4. The analyst must allow himself to appreciate the complexity of the emotional experience he is required to illuminate and yet restrict his choice to these three links. He decides what the linked objects are and which of these three represents with most accuracy the actual link between them.

If the patient is friendly the link can be represented by L. It is not an adequate representation because it is necessary to record the state of the transference. I save the trouble of saying what I mean by that by recording transference in accordance with the system I suggested earlier (p. 40, para. 6).

It will be seen that the use of HKL, to force the analyst to establish the "key" of the session is not the same as using it to record an emotional experience; that is to say it is a usage that provides a less than full account of what is known to have happened. But it introduces an element that must be an essential part of any recording system before that system can be regarded as satisfactory, namely the working tool. To sum up an emotional episode as K is to produce an imperfect record but a good starting point for the analyst's speculative meditation. In this respect the system I have sketched out, despite its crudity and naivety, possesses the rudiments of the essentials of a system of notation—record of fact and working tool.

CHAPTER FIFTEEN

1. THE AIM IN MAKING the choice L, H or K is to make one statement that is to the best of the analyst's belief true. It need not be a statement that accurately represents a realization of which it is the counterpart; the statement must seem to the analyst to be a true reflection of his feelings and one on which he can rely for a particularly important purpose, namely to act as a standard to which he can refer all the other statements that he proposes to make. If L is chosen then L expresses a quality with which he compares other qualities. L also expresses quantity and by this quantity the analyst will measure all the other quantities he expresses. That is to say, if he means by L that the two objects are linked by strong feelings of love he will not then use K for a casual tie such as might be expressed by an impatient "Yes, I know". The choice of L or H or K is not determined by a need to represent fact but by the need to provide a key to the value of the other elements that are combined in the formalized statement. In psycho-analysis where a statement depends on other statements for its value the need for the recognition of such a key statement is pressing. It must be made clear that the analyst is basing the values of all the elements in his statement on the one statement. Theoretically I see no reason why he should not choose any element he likes for this purpose, but in practice much is to be said for choosing an element that has importance derived from other aspects of its position in the total statement. Obviously an element which has already such importance is more likely to support the burden that it must carry than one that has not. The L, H or K link is just such an element. When the analyst chooses his sign it must feel right and, it stands to reason,

he must keep it constant. If by reference to it other elements seem to make the statement incompatible with itself the other elements and relationships must be brought into harmony and the L, H or K left unaltered unless it becomes clear that it has been wrongly chosen or that the analysand has changed; in that case the whole statement will have to be abandoned and a fresh start made. It will be seen that I attach great importance to the choice of L, H or K; that I have a preference for choosing the sign representing the link as the element best suited to carry the load I wish it to bear, but have no difficulty in conceiving that there might be good reasons why an analyst should prefer to make his "true" statement one based on some different element; I do not think the choice presents any unreasonable degree of difficulty to a trained and practising analyst.

2. L, H or K have to be decided in such a way that the analyst *feels* he has established a point of reference. By doing so the danger of producing a system of abstractions, devoid of background and subject only to ingenious and arbitrary manipulation, is made less.

CHAPTER SIXTEEN

THE K LINK

1. I SHALL IGNORE L and H and discuss K as it is important
for the analyst and is the link that is germane to learning by
experience. In the course of discussing it I hope also to take
up further points which are relevant to linking but with
which I have not so far been able to deal. My first point is
that L or H may be relevant to K but that neither is by
itself conducive to K. x K y, the analyst K the analysand,
I K Smith, these are statements that represent an emotional
experience. Like L and H, K represents an active link and
has about it a suggestion that if x K y then x does something
to y. It represents a psycho-analytic relationship. As I
propose to use it it does not convey a sense of finality, that
is to say, a meaning that x is in possession of a piece of
knowledge called y but rather that x is in the state of getting
to know y and y is in a state of getting to be known by x.
The statement x K y, in so far as it means that x has a piece
of knowledge called y, falls in the category of a relationship
between the person making the statement and the person to
whom it is made *and* a relationship with x and y about whom
it is made.

2. In so far as it is a statement meaning x is concerning
himself to know the truth about y it corresponds to statements
of relationship that are said to be informed by a scientific
outlook. The techniques employed by those who have a
scientific outlook have achieved most success when y is an
inanimate object. The conviction that a scientific outlook
prevails in the relationship x K y is more easily maintained
if y is inanimate and if x can be made to seem to approximate
to the inanimate, for example x uses a machine. Truth value

is felt to inhere in the record presented by a smoked drum or the record of the human voice in a way that is not felt to be the case in the report of human judgment. The simplicity of this view is exposed on occasions when it is believed that a photographic record cannot yield the evidence available to direct observation.

3. Doubts about human capacity to know anything underlie the inquiries of the philosopher of science; these doubts today spring from an inescapable awareness that the situation represented by these abstract terms x K y is identical with x L y or x H y in that an animate element exists intrinsically. That is to say that in proportion as inanimate machinery is introduced to displace the living element, L, H or K have ceased to exist. The problem with which philosophers of science have become associated has been given added significance by psycho-analysis and this for two main sets of reasons: x has the strength and is shown in detail to have the weakness of which he has always been suspected when he embarks on an investigation of y that is related to y's capacity for contact with reality. I do not propose to spend time on the philosophical problems involved as they can be found dealt with in Kant, Hume and their successors. I wish to emphasize that all that has been said about the problems of knowledge applies with particular force to psycho-analysis and that psycho-analysis applies with particular force to those problems.

4. The question "How can x know anything?" expresses a feeling; it appears to be painful and to inhere in the emotional experience that I represent by x K y. An emotional experience that is felt to be painful may initiate an attempt either to evade or to modify the pain according to the capacity of the personality to tolerate frustration. Evasion or modification in accordance with the view expressed by Freud in his paper on Two Principles of Mental Functioning are intended to remove the pain. Modification is attempted by using the relationship x K y so that it will lead to a relationship in which x is possessed of a piece of knowledge called y—the meaning for x K y repudiated by me on p. 47. Evasion on the other hand is attempted by substitution of the meaning

"x is possessed of a piece of knowledge called y" so that x K y no longer represents the painful emotional experience but the supposedly painless one.

5. Such a manœuvre is intended not to affirm but to deny reality, not to represent an emotional experience but to mis-represent it to make it appear to be a fulfilment rather than a striving for fulfilment. The difference between the aim of the lie and the aim of truth can thus be expressed as a change of sense in x K y and to relate to intolerance of the pain associated with feelings of frustration. The problem of trans-lating private "knowledge" into public is the same for mis-representing an emotional experience as it is for representing it. In the psycho-analysis of certain patients we have to concern ourselves with their failure to misrepresent emotional experiences even to themselves; it is possible to increase understanding of the insane by considering his failure to substitute a misrepresentation of the facts for the representa-tion that corresponds to, and therefore illuminates, reality. The motive is likely to be explained in Freud's statement that "hallucination was abandoned only in consequence of the absence of the expected gratification". It will be neces-sary to approach the problem as if with two distinct aims, one concerned with knowing a person or thing, K in fact, and the other concerned with evasion of K and the emotional experience it represents. The procedure I am proposing, as part of K for the purpose of knowing "x K y" and what it represents therefore involves identification with a person that comes for analysis. It also involves abstraction from the realization to produce a formulation that represents the realization and might therefore correspond with and so represent realizations at present unknown.

CHAPTER SEVENTEEN

1. In the K activity on which I am engaged, namely in knowing, I have to be conscious of my emotional experience and able to abstract from it a statement that will represent this experience adequately. This abstraction engenders confidence if it then represents other experiences unknown when the abstraction is made. The sense of confidence is similar to that produced if a belief seems supported by common sense. Confidence is a concomitant of knowing that there is correlation between the senses (p. 51) or that more than one person in a group entertains what appears to be the same statement of the same representation of an emotional experience. Confidence in a representation is associated with (1) a belief that the representation is supported by common sense and (2) that it not only represents the emotional experience from which it is abstracted, but represents other realizations, unknown when the abstraction was accomplished. Thus an abstract formalization, employing the signs LH and K used for the evaluation of one emotional experience may itself be evalued if it can be seen to serve as an abstract representation of a different emotional experience.

2. Abstraction, then, can be seen as a step in publication which facilitates correlation by comparison of the representation that has been abstracted with a number of different realizations none of which is the realization from which the representation was originally abstracted. The concretization, by contrast, can be seen as a form of publication which facilitates correlation by common sense; that is, by stating something so that it is recognized as an object of one sense that can yet be tested as an object of another sense. The criterion for the statement must be its value in facilitating testing by

more than one sense or by the senses of more than one person. (In astronomy correlations are achieved although only the sense of sight and its data are available because the individual discoverer has been able to make his private experience public for testing by other observers contemporary or post-humous. The weakness incidental to an inability to employ the evidence of more than one sense has been compensated for by the ability to abstract a statement of an original emotional experience in terms of such rigour that realizations of the representation could be sought for, found, or accidentally recognized many years afterwards. The intuition of heliocentricity of Aristarchus could be confirmed hundreds of years later by Kepler.) Mathematical formulation is not yet available to the psycho-analyst though there are suggestive possibilities.

3. The reasons for making an abstract statement are these; (1) the analyst is impelled to formulate his basic hypothesis; (2) the analyst is able to detect from the record that such abstraction makes available any tendency for the theoretical armoury on which he relies to become jejeune; (3) the analyst is preserved from losing sight of the provenance of his theoretical equipment in the history of his scientific discipline; (4) the analytic practitioners will be able more readily to see that certain theories hitherto regarded as established have in fact become redundant or discredited by the test of experience itself, and (5) correlation of the abstract statement with realizations from which it was *not* derived becomes possible; (6) it helps to establish a standard to which all other statements can be referred. Examples will be seen in the later pages.

The process of abstraction to which I have made conscious resort is essential to the x K y emotional experience. It is not an incidental procedure which can be discarded at will.

4. Once we have given priority to the link and agreed to limit its representation to the three signs L, H and K, it is possible to approach the problem of representation by considering what steps would be needed to establish a successful method of *mis*representation. Since the process of abstraction is not incidental and one to be discarded at will

positive steps have to be taken for an individual to achieve the state of mind, seen in some psychotics, in which the capacity for abstraction is destroyed. The value, for example, of the word dog which does not refer to a specific animal but to a class, as a method of achieving abstraction and generalization, is destroyed so that it can no longer be used as the name of a thing but is the thing in itself, "words are things". In a formalized system, designed to represent the K link it is necessary to introduce elements that will represent mis-representation. This can be done quite simply by borrowing from algebraic geometry the procedure by which a change of sign, say for a line AB represents a change in sense of the line. K represents the link I have adumbrated: — K represents the link constituted by NOT understanding i.e. *mis*-understanding. The implications of this can best be grasped by noting that — L is not the same as H, nor — H the same as L.

5. For the present factors must be represented by a page and line reference to that part of the literature that gives the best definition of the factor to which reference is being made. The search for signs to represent factors thus following the procedure I have adopted with L, H and K, is premature because substitution of a sign for an ordinarily accepted term produces a formalized system so divorced from its background that it becomes meaningless whereas by keeping to a system of page and line reference the background of realization from which the theories are derived is never wholly lost to sight. Formalization and abstraction on the other hand have the effect, by removing the concrete and particular, of eliminating aspects that obscure the importance of the relationship of one element with another. The employment of specific terms notable for their concreteness though retaining the background from which they are derived obscures the fact that concrete terms are variables dependent for their value on the context in which they are placed. This means that the essential thing is to find a set of signs that will adequately represent a realization and also make it possible to display the relationship of one sign with another—its context.

CHAPTER EIGHTEEN

1. IN THE WORK DONE HERE (K activity) I have resorted to abstraction, in contrast to that reverse process of concretization by which words cease to be abstract signs but become things themselves. To demonstrate relationship adequately abstraction and formalization are essential.

2. The problem is not merely the use of words already invested with a penumbra of associations to describe an unprecedented situation; it is that this penumbra of associations has been acquired in pursuit of the establishment of a mental relationship with concrete objects. This pursuit, in the development of the individual, is far less exacting than the attempt to establish a mental relationship with a personality either the individual's own or that of another person. The senses present the personality with material on which work has to be done to produce what Freud calls the "conscious awareness attached to them", that is to the sense data. But it is hard to believe that sense data, as ordinarily understood, could bring much material of value when the object of the senses is an emotional experience of a personality (to whomever it may belong). The senses may be able in a state of fear or rage to contribute data concerning the heart-beat, and similar events peripheral, as we see it, to an emotional state. But there are no sense-data directly related to psychic quality, as there are sense-data directly related to concrete objects. Hypochondriacal symptoms may therefore be signs of an attempt to establish contact with psychic quality by substituting physical sensation for the missing sense data of psychical quality. It seems possible that it was in response to his awareness of this difficulty that Freud felt disposed to postulate consciousness as the sense-organ of

psychic quality. I have no doubt whatever of the need for something in the personality to make contact with psychic quality.

3. For personalities that seem to be incapable of true dreaming, the border-line psychotic and psychotic parts of the personality, the theory of consciousness as the sense-organ of psychic quality is not satisfactory; by the standards of clinical practice contradictions become apparent which are resolved if the problems are approached with a different theory. The weakness of this theory of consciousness is manifest in the situation for which I have proposed the theory that alpha-function, by proliferating alpha-elements, is producing the contact-barrier, an entity that separates elements so that those on one side are, and form, the conscious and on the other side are, and form, the unconscious. The theory of consciousness is weak, not false, because by amending it to state that the conscious and the unconscious thus constantly produced together do function as if they were binocular therefore capable of correlation and self-regard. Because of the manner of its genesis, impartial register of psychic quality of the self is precluded: the "view" of one part by the other is, as it were, "monocular". For these reasons, and others arising from clinical experience of psychoanalysis of that class of patient in whom the psychotic part of the personality is obtrusive, I find the theory of primary and secondary processes unsatisfactory. This theory is weak in the need to postulate two systems at the point where, in my theory of an alpha-function, an emotional experience is transformed into alpha-elements,[1] to make dream thought, unconscious waking thinking and storage in the mind (memory) possible. I attribute the appearance of beta-elements, the closely associated bizarre objects and the serious disturbances ordinarily associated with excessive obtrusion of the psychotic elements of the personality, to the failure of alpha-function.

CHAPTER NINETEEN

1. ATTRIBUTION OF A VALUE to the term alpha-function is a task of psycho-analysis and can be achieved in no other way. Its status, as I discuss it here, is that of an unknown variable to be used to satisfy the need for a system of abstraction adequate to the requirements of psycho-analysis. This and related problems are objects of the enquiry; they are also instruments by which the enquiry is conducted.[1] A distinction must be made between the concept of alpha-function and the realization which is felt to approximate sufficiently closely to the theory in which this concept is employed to warrant appropriation of the term alpha-function as a name, however temporary, for the realization.

2. The genesis of all abstraction is to be supposed, for purposes of analytic investigation, to be a factor in alpha-function. Such an hypothesis is compatible with the association of breakdown in alpha-function with predominance of beta-elements which are remarkable for their concreteness to a point where some patients regard words not as the names of things but as things-in-themselves. The hypothesis must be matched against emotional experiences that are a part of the clinical problem of establishing a value for alpha-function itself. First we need to know what is the counterpart of a sense impression in the relationship of a person with an emotional experience. The sense-organs, the awareness belonging to them and their realizations derive from the sensuous experience of concrete objects. What deals with the counterparts of a sense impression of an emotional experience? How are these counterparts of a sense impression then transformed into alpha-elements? It is helpful to postulate[1] sense impressions of an emotional experience

55

analogous to sense impressions of concrete objects. If there
are such impressions we shall have to consider whether the
alpha-elements into which alpha-function transforms the
sense impressions of an emotional experience differ from the
alpha-elements into which alpha-function transforms the
sense-data of a concrete object and if so in what the difference
consists. Freud suggested that the model for primary and
secondary processes was the reflex apparatus; the application of the theory of functions requires that the model is
formed first, and then inspected to see if it can be represented
by the theoretical abstraction I have called a link and if it
can represent, and if so how, the realization that has stimulated the production of the model. Alpha-function represents
something that exists when certain factors operate in consort.
It is assumed that there are factors which operate in such
consort or alternatively that if for some reason they do not,
that is to say that if the available factors have no alpha-
function, then the personality is incapable of producing
alpha-elements and therefore incapable of dream thoughts,
consciousness or unconsciousness, repression, or learning
from experience. This failure is serious because in addition
to the obvious penalties that follow from an inability to learn
from experience there is a need for awareness of an emotional
experience, similar to the need for an awareness of concrete
objects that is achieved through the sense impressions,
because lack of such awareness implies a deprivation of truth
and truth seems to be essential for psychic health. The effect
on the personality of such deprivation is analogous to the
effect of physical starvation on the physique.

3. By resorting to abstraction and its products, alpha-
function and its factors, I have been able to discuss psycho-
analytic unknowns. I continue by concretization, that is,
by using terms approximating to those used on a level of
empirically verifiable data, to speculate on what part of the
early psychic apparatus it is that is deflected to the provision
of the apparatus needed for thought. Freud, describing
thought as providing a method of restraint for motor discharge which had become necessary, simply says it developed
from ideation. In his discussion of dream interpretation

Freud was impressed by the value of reflex apparatus as a model for the psychic apparatus involved in dreaming and evolved his theory of primary and secondary systems in the light of this model.[1] I suggest that thinking is something forced on an apparatus, not suited for the purpose, by the demands of reality, and is contemporary with, as Freud said, the dominance of the reality principle. A modern analogy is provided by the fact that the demands of reality not only forced the discovery of psycho-analysis, but have led to the deflection of verbal thought from its original function of providing restraint for motor discharge to the tasks of self knowledge for which it is ill-suited and for the purpose of which it has to undergo drastic changes.

4. It will be seen that I ignore the nature of alpha-function and leave it as an abstraction for use as an unknown that is given a value only in the course of an analytic investigation.[1] I am therefore tackling a different problem from that which Freud investigated with his theories of ideation and his model of the reflex arc. I am assuming that an apparatus existed and had to undergo, still has to undergo, adaptation to the new tasks involved in meeting the demands of reality by developing a capacity for thought. The apparatus that has to undergo this adaptation is that which dealt originally with sense impressions relating to the alimentary canal.

In this system, as far as I can make out and as far as I am able to render what I have deduced in words, what takes place is this; the infant is aware of a very bad breast inside it, a breast that is "not there" and by not being there gives it painful feelings. This object is felt to be "evacuated" by the respiratory system or by the process of "swallowing" a satisfying breast. This breast that is swallowed is indistinguishable from a "thought" but the "thought" is dependent on the existence of an object that is actually put into the mouth. In certain conditions, dependent on factors of the personality, the sucking process and its attendant sensations are equated with evacuation of the bad breast. The breast, the thing in itself, is indistinguishable from an idea in the mind. The idea of a breast in the mind is, reciprocally, indistinguishable from the thing itself in the mouth. Keeping for the present to two situations only, one of which is an actual breast, indistinguishable from an emotional experience which in turn is thing-in-itself and thought, but in an undifferentiated state, and the other the bad "need-of-a-breast" bad breast which is equally an object compounded of emotional experience and thing-in-itself the two being as yet undifferentiated, it is clear that we have arrived at an object very closely resembling a beta-element. The realization and the representation of it in the mind have not been differentiated. The characteristics of this condition may be made clearer if I educe some manifestations of it. Thus an infant containing a "need-of-a-breast" bad breast may evacuate it by sucking at the breast. This obviously requires a topographically close relationship with an actual breast. It may evacuate it by the respiratory system; there need be no tactile sensation for this. It may evacuate it by seeing the actual breast; for this an actual breast needs to be in sight, that is to say it is in a position in which being in sight is the same as being in the mind's eye and both are the same as being in the mouth. When all these events are evacuations of the "need-of-a-breast" bad breast it is clear that if no breast is then in fact available the "no breast" will be felt to be not only bad in itself but made worse because it, as it were, is concrete evidence that this bad breast has been successfully evacuated. This situation corresponds to one in which a "bizarre object" rather than a "beta-element" would be the correct descriptive term for the object felt by the infant to exist.

CHAPTER TWENTY

1. WHEN EVACUATION of a bad breast is felt to lead to its presence externally, if the evacuation is achieved, apparently by sucking at a real breast, the aftermath of the evacuation is not painful as in the respiratory and other methods. This stimulates interaction between the reality and pleasure-pain principles. We may follow-up (1) the process of differentiation of the representation from the corresponding realization, the process by which the thing in itself is distinguishable from the idea, (Bradley, I.148) or (2) the effects of the correspondence between alimentation and thinking. The first course leads directly to a discussion of the importance of abstraction, which may, in this context, be regarded as an aspect of the transformation, by alpha-function, of an emotional experience into alpha-elements.

2. The Kleinian theory that the infant feels it has evacuated its bad object into the breast combined with the theory that satisfaction of a need can be felt as evacuation of a need, the need itself being a bad breast (to employ concrete terms) or what I have called a beta-element (to employ an abstraction) represents an infant's feeling that the breast in actuality is an evacuated object and therefore indistinguishable from a beta-element. Something must happen now if the child is to continue feeding. It is implied in the process I have described that the situation cannot be recognized as objective. If there is a good breast, a sweet object, it is because it has been evacuated, produced; and the same with the bad breast, the needed breast, the bitter breast, etc. It cannot be seen as objective and it cannot be seen as subjective. From these sweet, bitter, sour objects, sweetness, bitterness, sourness, are abstracted. Once abstracted they can be reapplied;

the abstraction made can be used in situations where a realization, not the original realization from which it was abstracted, approximates to it. For example an emotional experience is associated with the breast, in which the infant feels that there is an object existing independently of itself on which it can depend for satisfaction of its feelings of hunger; assuming a capacity for abstraction, the infant can feel that from the total experience he can detach an element which is a belief that an object exists that can satisfy his needs. The concrete statement might be: a breast exists that can be depended on to satisfy his hunger for food; abstraction from this might be: there is a something that can and does give him what he wants when he wants it.

3. Almost any number of statements can be made to represent what the infant feels when, in the view of a reputedly impartial observer, it has been fed at the breast. From that emotional experience and the statement that represents it, and all the other statements that could equally reasonably be felt to represent it, there can be abstracted a series of further statements. Since an enormous number can be made, the significance of this for scientific procedure, with particular reference to this preceding passage, will be discussed later. Presumably the infant also "can make a number of statements" and that it is with the nature of these "statements" that the analyst has ultimately to concern himself. The first level of statements are particular, derived from an actual episode, and concrete; the abstractions become further and further removed from the concrete and specific until their origin is lost to sight. The abstractions that are thus produced may then be reapplied to a realization when a realization is found that appears to approximate to the abstraction.

4. Situations met with in analysis are: (1) a patient, incapable of abstraction, strives to exist with a mental apparatus engaged in introjection and projection of beta-elements; (2) a patient capable of abstraction produces theoretical systems far removed from the background of realizations from which they have been abstracted, but proliferates these systems according to rules that make the abstractions in any system consistent with each other; (3) a

patient capable of producing abstractions proliferates systems
that seem to obey no ascertainable system of rules. Though
the original realization is unknown (in this respect resembling
(2) above) and likewise the system of rules under which the
abstractions have been manipulated, he may yet find
realizations that approximate to his abstract statements;
(4) a patient capable of abstraction and formation of systems
in accordance with rules that ensure that the system is not
incompatible with itself and yet unable to find a realization
to which the abstract systems apply; (5) a patient capable
of abstraction and of combining these abstractions into
systems according to rules (whose nature can be demon-
strated) that ensure that the systems are not incompatible
with themselves. It may be possible to deduce what the
original realization was from which the abstraction was
derived. Further realizations can be seen to approximate
to the deductive systems although the latter realizations may
not have been known to exist when the abstraction that can
be seen to represent them was first adumbrated.

5. I shall ignore (1) as it is a statement whose derived
abstract systems form representations of realizations that are
usually felt to be of a different kind from the realizations
corresponding with (2), (4), (5). (3) represents a realization
which we shall have to consider further. It is peculiar in
that realizations approximating to this representation bear
a superficial resemblance to the realizations approximating
to (1) and other realizations approximating to the representations derived from (1).

6. Throughout discussion of (1), (2), (3), (4) and (5),
abstraction may be usefully investigated as a factor in alpha-
function. There are two tasks on which it is now necessary
to embark. The first is the elucidation of original realizations
of the abstraction. The second task is to elucidate the relationship of the model (as Freud uses the term in the passage
in which he refers to the reflex apparatus as being the model
for the apparatus involved in dreaming) to the realization
from which the abstraction and the theoretical deductive
systems have been derived; to what extent and in what
circumstances can this original realization be seen to be, or

used as, a model for the abstraction derived from it? It can easily be used as such a model unwittingly. For example, I have spoken of certain locutions as being evidence not for memory but for "undigested facts" (p. 7). Implicit in this statement is the use of the alimentary system as a model for the processes of thought. There is reason to believe that the emotional experiences associated with alimentation are those from which individuals have abstracted and then integrated elements to form theoretical deductive systems that are used as representations of realizations of thought. There is reason for using alimentary system as a model for demonstrating and comprehending the processes involved in thought. No objection, except on grounds of inefficacy, can be raised against the procedure as one by which the original realization and the emotional experience to which it gave rise is transformed to provide representations for realizations that seem to approximate to them. Moreover the concrete image of the original realization can be used as a model for a subsequent realization. The distinction between the representation, formed from alpha-elements combined to produce an abstract theoretical deductive system, and a model formed from concrete images combined according to what were conceived to be the relationships between the components of the original realization, is important and must be preserved to avoid confusion. But what is to be said for using our knowledge of the alimentary system to form a model, not for the processes involved in thought but for the processes involved in thought about thought?

7. Problems associated with disturbance of thought compel us to think about thought and this raises a question of technique—*how* are we to think about thought—what is the correct method? It is clear that we can use our knowledge of the alimentary canal unwittingly when we are concerned to elucidate disorders of thought and therefore phenomena that are related to the patient's attitude to, and his capacity for, thinking about thought. The importance of this question lies in the fact that certain patients are influenced by the belief that they digest thoughts and that the consequences of doing so are similar to the digestion of food. That is to

say that if they attempt what might ordinarily be regarded as meditating on an idea, they believe that the thoughts so treated suffer a change analogous to that undergone by food that is turned into faeces: some ideas, or their verbal representations, survive and if expressed emerge not as evidence of the possession of an idea, but as evidence, embedded in a matrix of gibberish, that their thoughts have been destroyed and denuded of meaning in the way that faeces and its undigested particles can be regarded as food that has been destroyed and denuded of its value as food.[1] Interpretations addressed to such a patient need to be couched in terms that avoid words in which the model of the alimentary system is implicit. In practice if the difficulty is recognized by the analyst steps can be taken to prevent making the confusion worse confounded. But the problem stimulates the thought that unconscious employment of this model may be creating difficulties not only for the psychotic but also for the philosopher of science who is engaged on problems of methods of clear thinking. The term "clear thinking" that I have just employed is itself evidence of the extent to which the vocabulary of philosophy and of psycho-analysis, which may be regarded as having a relationship to philosophy analogous to the relationship of mathematics to applied mathematics, is saturated with models derived from sense impressions of material objects. We may thus resort unaware to the same methods of understanding, and that includes representing realizations in the realms of thought by the models employed in the original realization. It is true that the model with which present knowledge of the alimentary canal provides us will be very different from the model with which the infant's knowledge of the alimentary system provides him. A similar difference applies to the systems built on the alpha-elements that are derived as part of the process of abstraction; the infant's abstractions are not those of the adult.

CHAPTER TWENTY-ONE

1. THE USE OF A MODEL has a value in restoring a sense of the concrete to an investigation which may have lost contact with its background through abstraction and the theoretical deductive systems associated with it. Its merit in this respect is matched by its merit as a primitive approach to abstraction in that a whole experience, say feeding, is being used as a model for a later problem. The defect of the model as an instrument adds force to the need to produce abstractions.

2. A model has also qualities which enable it to fulfil some of the functions of an abstraction. It enables the investigator to use an emotional experience by applying it as a totality, to a subsequent experience, or to some aspect of it. These merits carry in themselves the elements that finally make the model outdated. No experience exactly matches a past experience; scientific deductive system and its abstractions, or the model and its associated images, can only be an approximation to the realization and vice versa.

3. I distinguish between the model and the abstraction by reserving the term model for a construction in which concrete images are combined with each other; the link between concrete images often gives the effect of a narrative implying that some elements in the narrative are the causes of others. It is constructed with elements from the individual's past, whereas the abstraction is, as it were, impregnated with preconceptions of the individual's future.[1] Its similarity with the model lies in its origin in an emotional experience and its application to a fresh emotional experience; its dissimilarity lies in the gain in flexibility and applicability which is obtained by loss of particular concrete images; the elements in the abstraction are not combined by narrative

but by a method intended to reveal the relationship rather than the objects related. The deductive system abstracts from an emotional experience those qualities that display the relationship between the elements in that emotional experience. The actual elements related are of lesser consequence. The model stresses the actual elements, the visual images, but the manner in which they are strung together is of subordinate significance.

4. The fact that any realization only approximates to the representation, be it abstraction or model, is the stimulus for further abstraction and further model making.

If the learner is intolerant of the essential frustration of learning he indulges phantasies of omniscience and a belief in a state where things are known. Knowing something consists in "having" some "piece of" knowledge and *not* in what I have called K.

The description of model making and abstraction in Chapters 20 and 21 is itself an example of model making and abstraction employed in K (or "knowing" in the sense of "getting to know" something). If the model making and abstraction imply a capacity for alpha-function they are compatible with all the states of mind mentioned on p. 60 except (1). If there is evidence of (1) the incompatibility of (1) with the others means that (1) and (2), (3), (4), etc. co-exist but are split off from each other.

CHAPTER TWENTY-TWO

1. THE WRITING OF THIS BOOK is a realization of K. The difficulties of the patient suffering from a "disorder of thought" are similar to those that beset scientists, and others concerned with the establishment of facts, in that they arise through failure to ascertain facts and so involve investigation of the nature of the failure. The failure of patients suffering from disorders of thought is patently within the personality. Psychoanalysis of that failure is impossible without understanding the problem of the philosopher of science and conversely his problem is incompletely stated without the aid of psychoanalytic experience of disorders of thought.[1] Investigation of abstraction as a part of the psycho-analytic armoury will be by this two-fold approach. I shall first discuss abstraction as a factor of alpha-function in a K-link.

2. Let us suppose the infant repeats an emotional experience in which the following elements are constantly conjoined; the sight of a man, a sense of being loved by the man, a sense of wanting the man, an awareness of the repetition of a phrase, by the mother, of "That's Daddy." "Da, da, da" says the child. "That's right; Daddy" says the mother. From the emotional experience the infant abstracts certain elements, what they are depending partly on the infant; these abstracted elements are given a name "Daddy" in other situations in which the same elements appear to be conjoined; thus a vocabulary is established. This is not a description of fact; I give it the status of a model from which I abstract a theory and expect to find that it is a representation to which some realization corresponds. The theory I abstract is: "Daddy" is the name of an hypothesis.[1] The

hypothesis called "Daddy" is a statement that certain
elements are constantly conjoined.

3. The infant now meets another who also says Da-da-da,
but in circumstances that do not appear to correspond with
the circumstances with which Da-da-da is associated. There
is a man, but it is the wrong one. Yet elements in this new
situation correspond with elements in situations that the
infant regards as realizations corresponding to the hypothesis
of which the name is "Daddy". The hypothesis must be
revised to represent the realizations. It may be abandoned
for another or it may become a system of hypothesis, a
scientific deductive system. The experiences continue and
the scientific deductive system named "Daddy" becomes
progressively more complex. Using the model to abstract a
theory, the individual must be capable of abstracting from
an emotional experience elements that appear to be constantly conjoined including one element which is at one and
the same time the name of the theory or hypothesis or
scientific deductive system; it is also the name of the realization that is believed to approximate to the theory. Thus,
"chair" is: (1) the name given to a thing in itself, as it is
supposed to exist in actuality; this, following Kant, cannot
be known to us.[1] (2) the name given to the selected fact. (3)
the name given to a selection of feelings, impressions, etc.,
that are felt, by virtue of the selected fact, to be related and
coherent. (4) the name of the definitory hypothesis that
states that these elements are constantly conjoined. (3) and
(4) correspond to Kant's secondary and primary qualities.
These distinctions of the nature of the content of the term
"chair" are of practical importance to psycho-analysts who
face the necessity for, and difficulty of, communication within
the group. So far I have used only two words, Daddy and
chair, as examples of names of hypotheses i.e. of elements
abstracted from an emotional situation and given coherence
by the name.

4. The use of the term hypothesis as a name for the
object that would more often be described as a concept is
an expression of the problem presented by (3) as it
emerges when investigated psycho-analytically. The problem

presented by the psycho-analytic experience is the lack of any adequate terminology to describe it and in this respect it resembles the problem that Aristotle solved by supposing that mathematics dealt with mathematical objects. It is convenient to suppose that psycho-analysis deals with psycho-analytic objects and that it is with the detection and observation of these objects that the psycho-analyst must concern himself in the conduct of an analysis. (3) describes an aspect of these objects. I employ the term hypothesis provisionally because the meaning associated with the scientific use of this term has aspects that are shared by the psycho-analytic object. The identification of such an object depends on (*a*) the possibility of finding a means by which the nature of the object can be communicated. This involves the employment of the very methods that are the object of this investigation, and (*b*) the mental equipment that the observer can bring to bear. Both (*a*) and (*b*) are therefore adumbrations of problems on which these investigations must converge.

5. From all the elements in a realization only some have their corresponding sense data linked with each other as being constantly conjoined. These elements, and their corresponding sense data may therefore be regarded as abstracted from the totality of elements in the realization. A further abstraction takes place when the elements are given a name that is perceived to be different from the realization it represents. The abstraction must be capable of fulfilling the function of a pre-conception. The generalization must therefore be capable of particularization; the abstraction must be capable of concretization. Implicit in the term concretization is the model from which it is derived. The model supplies a background of meaning that can preserve my statement from being so far divorced from reality as to become unsuited for mating with its realization. But the implication that is its strength becomes a weakness when it is employed by a participant in a relationship in which the link is minus K. (Henceforward I shall write this " — K"; it is discussed in detail in Chapter 28). This weakness and its exploitation in — K becomes apparent in analysis of the patient who appears to be unable to abstract, the patient to whom words

are things—*the* things which the word is supposed to represent, but which are for him indistinguishable from their
name and vice versa.

6. The problems associated with abstraction may be
illuminated if regarded in reverse as problems of movement
from the general to the particular, the abstract to the concrete. When I speak of concretization I employ, and hope
to be understood to employ, a metaphor. This class of
patient would not understand that. For him the word would
be a lump of concrete.[1] This would equally be true if he tried
as I am trying, to make my meaning clear by employing
the term concretization. I can be aware of failing to make
my meaning clear but I do not think my difficulty lies in
passing lumps of concrete when what I want is to talk.

7. The theory that the concept is a statement that certain
elements are constantly conjoined and that the word is the
name of that statement, can be used as a model to formulate
a more abstract and widely embracing theory. The realization of every emotional situation is an approximation to a
theoretical deductive system that represents it, even though
that scientific deductive system or representation has not
been discovered.

8. It is now possible to formulate the nature of a psycho-
analytical object more easily. Suppose ψ represents a constant, (ξ) an unsaturated element that determines the value
of the constant once it has been identified. We may use the
unknown constant ψ to represent an inborn pre-conception.
Employing a model to give temporary meaning to the term
"inborn pre-conception" I shall suppose that an infant has
an inborn pre-conception that a breast that satisfies its own
incomplete nature exists. The realization of the breast
provides an emotional experience. This experience corresponds to Kant's secondary and primary qualities of a phenomenon. The secondary qualities determine the value of the
unsaturated element (ξ) and therefore the value of ψ (ξ).
This sign now represents a conception. The previously unsaturated element (ξ) together with the unknown constant
ψ share a component, that is the inborn character of
the personality. Let that be represented by $(\mathcal{M})$. The

psycho-analytic object may then be represented by ψ (ξ) $(\mathcal{M})$. The value of $(\mathcal{M})$, as of (ξ), is determined by the emotional experience stimulated by the realization, that is, in the model I have put forward, by the contact with the breast. The value of the psycho-analytic object ψ (ξ) $(\mathcal{M})$ is then determined by the identification of (ξ) $(\mathcal{M})$ that is precipitated by a realization.

9. This is not all. The extension of the concept of a psycho-analytic object, like the extensions of all biological concepts, includes phenomena related to growth. Growth may be regarded as positive or negative. I shall represent it by $(\pm \, Y)$. The plus and minus signs are employed to give sense or direction to the element they precede in a manner analogous to their mode of employment in co-ordinate geometry. To indicate this aspect of its extension I shall represent the psycho-analytic object by $\{(\pm \, Y)\psi$ $(\mathcal{M})(\xi)\}$. Whether (Y) is preceded by plus or minus sign will be determined only by contact with a realization. Abstraction from the psycho-analytic object will be related to the resolution of the conflicting claims of narcissism and social-ism. If the trend is social $(+ \, Y)$ abstraction will be related to the isolation of primary qualities. If the trend is narcissistic $(- \, Y)$ abstraction will be replaced by activity appropriate to $- \, K$, which I have not yet discussed.

10. K, to which the analyst is restricted, involves abstraction from the psycho-analytic object represented by $\{(Y)\psi$ $(\xi)(\mathcal{M})\}$. The abstraction must be capable of serving as the constant so that it can fulfil the function of an unknown and yet, by virtue of the analytic object from which it derives, have the attributes of a preconception that has, unlike the inborn pre-conception, a penumbra of meaning. It remains an unknown, but the range of values which can be conferred upon it by the identification of (ξ) is restricted. The term "*a priori*" knowledge can only apply to psycho-analytic objects where ψ is an unknown whose value can be determined by identification of (ξ) without restriction.

It is necessary and should be possible to find hypotheses that may be used in scientific deductive systems as either premises or as derived hypotheses. These scientific deductive systems, abstracted from emotional experiences, may then be found to represent other emotional experiences from which they have not been derived, but which can be seen to approximate to the representative scientific deductive system in question. The scientific deductive system may then be further abstracted to yield the equivalent of an algebraic calculus which would represent it.

CHAPTER TWENTY-THREE

1. H. POINCARÉ DESCRIBES the process of creation of a mathematical formulation thus:

"If a new result is to have any value, it must unite elements long since known, but till then scattered and seemingly foreign to each other, and suddenly introduce order where the appearance of disorder reigned. Then it enables us to see at a glance each of these elements in the place it occupies in the whole. Not only is the new fact valuable on its own account, but it alone gives a value to the old facts it unites. Our mind is frail as our senses are; it would lose itself in the complexity of the world if that complexity were not harmonious; like the short-sighted, it would only see the details, and would be obliged to forget each of these details before examining the next, because it would be incapable of taking in the whole. The only facts worthy of our attention are those which introduce order into this complexity and so make it accessible to us."[1]

2. This description closely resembles the psycho-analytical theory of paranoid-schizoid and depressive positions adumbrated by Mrs. Klein. I have used the term "selected fact" to describe that which the psycho-analyst must experience in the process of synthesis. The name of one element is used to particularize the selected fact, that is to say the name of that element in the realization that appears to link together elements not hitherto seen to be connected. The representations of the selected facts may then be seen to have a similar coherence if the appropriate representation for a number of selected facts can be found. The selected facts, together with the selected fact that appears to give coherence to a number of selected facts, emerge from a psycho-analytic object or

series of such objects, but cannot be formulated in accordance with the principles governing a scientific deductive system. Before such a system can be created the selected facts have to be worked upon by conscious rational processes. Only then can the representation be formulated that will bring together the elements of coherent selected facts in a scientific deductive system. In the scientific deductive system the hypotheses of the system should be held together by rules but these do not correspond with that which, in the realization, appears to link together the elements whose relationship appears to be revealed by the selected fact. Now the rules that hold together the hypotheses in the system of hypotheses, namely the scientific deductive system, are the rules of logic. The relationship amongst the hypotheses of a scientific deductive system, namely the logical connection between them that has been brought into prominence by the deductive system, is characteristic of conscious rational thought but not of the relationship between the elements in a realization of which the phenomena appear to cohere as a result of the discovery of a selected fact. The selected fact is the name of an emotional experience, the emotional experience of a sense of discovery of coherence; its significance is therefore epistemological and the relationship of selected facts must not be assumed to be logical. The elements thought to be related have a counterpart in actuality of things-in-themselves. Are we to assume that the selected fact represents a thing-in-itself and similarly that the relationship, namely the logical relationship, between the elements in the deductive system has also a counterpart in actuality, a thing-in-itself that approximates to deductive logic? In fact the mathematical formulation has some of the characteristics of an attempt to formulate a system of relationships between mathematical objects to which some realization of relationships might approximate. In other words there is no reason why the rules governing the logical manipulation of the elements in a scientific deductive system should have any corresponding realization. It follows that the elements in an analytic object may be related to each other in a manner entirely different from the manner in which their representations are linked

in a scientific deductive system. Progress in elucidation of
the field of relatedness will probably depend on illumination
by K of — K and the psycho-analytic objects peculiar to
that.

3. The network of relationships discernible in the scientific deductive system or its corresponding calculus may not
have any realization and for the following reasons. Successful investigations have been associated with inanimate objects which the animate object shares with the inanimate.
In such cases the logical structure of the scientific deductive
system and the algebraic calculus representing it appears to
have a corresponding realization probably because it is
abstracted from a similar realization. That is to say there
is a realization that seems to correspond approximately to
the actual network of relationships that is internal to the
scientific deductive system itself. Investigation of elements
that are essentially animate does not yield such a correspondence. The form of association between elements bound
together by narrative is distinct from the form of association
discerned through transition from paranoid-schizoid to
depressive position.

4. The narrative form is associated with the theory of
causation and the other with the depressive positions and the
selected fact. There may be no realization that corresponds
with these two theories.

5. Any experience may be used as a "model" for some
future experience. This aspect of learning by experience
is related to, and may be identical with, the function Freud
attributes to attention when he says it had "periodically to
search the outer world in order that its data might be already
familiar if an urgent inner need should arise". The value
of a model is that its familiar data are available to meet
urgent inner or outer need. The selected fact precipitates
the model. The coherence of the elements in the model that
is identified with the realization is then felt to pertain to the
elements of the realization.

6. Before an emotional experience can be used for a
model its sense data have to be transformed into alpha-
elements to be stored and made available for abstraction.

(In — K the meaning is abstracted leaving a denuded representation.) Model making during the experience relates to the model needed for that experience; alpha-function during the experience provides the elements needed for model making in a subsequent experience; the model is precipitated during the experience for which the model is needed. Elements are removed from mental storage to provide a model that is an approximation to the event it is to illuminate. The personality abstracts from experience the elements expected to recur and forms from these elements the model that will preserve something of the original experience but with enough flexibility to permit adaptation to new but supposedly similar experiences. He abstracts elements to construct either a model or an abstraction or both. I shall use the term model where the construct is forged to meet an "urgent need" for concreteness. (Construct, forged, concreteness. All three words carry implications of the models from which the words have been abstracted. I have left the passage as an example of the latent, though in this case noticeable, influence of the model.) If the need is for a model those elements will be abstracted from the store of alpha-elements that have, like visual images, a reminiscence of the emotional experience during which the alpha-element was formed. The more such elements are employed the more rigid the model becomes and the more restricted its application; the restriction is modified if the model formed from a combination of these elements is then submitted to further abstraction. The abstractions need then to be combined in accordance with the rules of logic. This system of abstractions is the scientific deductive system.

CHAPTER TWENTY-FOUR

1. SUPPOSE THAT THE PATIENT has produced a number of associations and other material. The analyst has available:

(1) Observations of the patient's material;
(2) Various emotional experiences of his own;
(3) A knowledge of one or more versions of the myth of Oedipus[1];
(4) One or more versions of psycho-analytical theory of the Oedipus complex;
(5) Other fundamental psycho-analytic theories.

Some aspects of the session will appear familiar; they will remind him of past experiences analytical and otherwise. Others will seem to bear a resemblance to the oedipal situation. From these sources the analyst can form a model; the problem is to decide whether the analyst is confronted by a realization of Freud's theory of the oedipus complex. The Oedipus theory, does not correspond closely to what a physicist would call a scientific deductive system but can be formulated to qualify for inclusion in such a category. Its weakness as a member of this class is likely to be its lack of abstraction and the peculiar structure by which its elements are related to each other. In part this is due to the fact that the more concrete the elements the less they lend themselves to variation of combination.

2. In addition two factors (1) the actual nature of the network of relationships in which the elements are held, and (2) the derivation of the elements from a myth contrast with the elements in a scientific deductive system as used by a physicist. The latter purports to derive from one realization

and to be able to represent another, whereas the psycho-analytic formulation is derived from and expressed by the emotional experience of a folk narrative and is said to represent a realization encountered in psycho-analysis. Freud derived his theory from the emotional experience of psychoanalytic inquiry, but his description could not be comparable with the formulations usually supposed to represent scientific discovery. I wish to discuss only two methodological weaknesses in the Oedipus theory and these are:

(1) The theory as it stands is so concrete that it cannot be matched with its realization; that is to say no realization can be found to approximate to a theory whose elements, concrete in themselves, are combined in a narrative network of relationships that is intrinsic and essential. Without the narrative the elements lose their value.

Conversely:

(2) If the elements are generalized the theory becomes an ingenious manipulation of elements according to arbitrary rules—the commonest formulation of this suspicion of the theory is the criticism that analyst and analysand indulge a taste for jargon.

3. A theoretical formulation that appears to be too concrete and yet too abstract requires to be generalized in such a way that its realizations are more easily detected, without the attendant weakness, most often seen in mathematics, of appearing to be an arbitrary manipulation of symbols. Can it retain its concrete elements without losing flexibility so essential in psycho-analytic application? It can be made more abstract though we may not find an algebraic calculus to represent the scientific deductive system. I shall say more about this possibility later.

4. I am convinced of the strength of the scientific position of psycho-analytic practice. I believe that the practice of psycho-analysts in making psycho-analysis an essential training experience deals with the fundamental difficulties for the time being because it makes conscious and unconscious available for correlation; but I do not consider the need less

pressing to investigate the weaknesses that spring from faulty
theory construction, lack of notation and failure of methodical
care amd maintenance of psycho-analytic equipment.
("Care", "maintenance", "equipment",—again the implicit
model.)

CHAPTER TWENTY-FIVE

1. THE MODEL MAY BE REGARDED as an abstraction from an emotional experience or as a concretization of an abstraction. The latter has affinities with the transformation of an hypothesis into terms of empirically verifiable data. In the group the myth has some claim to be regarded as filling the same role in the society as the model has in scientific work of the individual.

2. As an example of a model I take the imaginary story of the infant learning the word Daddy. This story does not purport to be a fact. It is derived from experience of patients in analysis, observation of children, desultory reading, some of it philosophical, and other sources; in short it is derived from experience—*my* experience. It is an artefact composed of elements that have been selected by me from my store of experience. But it has been formed for a specific purpose; the selection and combination of elements is not fortuitous but is made to "explain" or illuminate the problem of abstraction. It has, therefore, no value as evidence; its value lies in the ease with which it can be communicated and compared with facts. By contrast the account of the patient who feels that words are things is not a model but an example; what I describe purports to be a realization. The model was made to illuminate the experience I had with a particular patient and is used for comparison with the realization. Potentially, every realization approximates to an abstraction or scientific deductive system even if one to which it corresponds has not yet been discovered (p. 61). When I compare model and realization it may result in my receiving the illumination I desire; it may prove so unrewarding that I assume the model is worthless and discard

79

it. Models are ephemeral and differ from theories in this respect; I have no compunction in discarding a model as soon as it has served or failed to serve my purpose. If a model proves useful on a number of different occasions the time has come to consider its transformation into a theory.

3. A psycho-analyst may make as many models as he chooses out of any material available to him. It is important not to confound these ephemeral structures with realizations on the one hand or theories on the other. The model has a valuable function provided always that it is recognized for what it is. If the analyst believes he is describing an actual event he should make this clear and should not allow the distinction between an event, for the authenticity of which there is supporting evidence, and a model to become blurred. The same applies to the distinction between a model and a theory. I shall deal with the peculiar difficulties that beset the psycho-analyst in avoiding confusion in making the distinction between theory and model and between a model and the particular form of theory known as a psycho-analytical interpretation.

4. The process of abstraction from a realization may proceed directly from realization to scientific deductive system through the intervening phase of model making. Elements are selected from the model and used as elements in the scientific deductive system. The need for this procedure becomes apparent when a model is used to illuminate a realization that is thought to approximate to the model and the model is then found to be insufficiently similar to clarify the problem for which a solution is sought. I ignore the contingency that arises when the realization is mistakenly matched with the model; that failure is dealt with by the creation of a new model. An important failure is that which arises when the model is seen to be the nearest possible approximation to the realization, but nevertheless fails to mirror developments in the realization by the movement in its own internal structure. This failure can occur whenever model making is used; but there must be heightened risk of its occurrence when, as in psycho-analysis, we are concerned with growth and speak of "mental mechanisms". To

talk of "mechanism" suggests that, whatever the phenomenon is that is thus described, it is likely that the implied
model is more suitable to the inanimate machine than to a
living organism. It is likely to emphasize those aspects of
the living organism which it shares with the inanimate. This
defect is serious because we require models when the problem
is most complex, that is when the characteristics of growth are
central; and that is most of the time. The term mechanism
implies the model of a machine which is precisely what the
realization is not. The dangers of too great abstraction do not
admit of an easy solution by discarding the use of models.
Psychoanalysts are therefore certain to become familiar with
the situation in which the model used to avoid the dangers of
theorising, in which I include interpretation, suffers from
the complementary defect of being so close to the realization
from which it is derived that it is correspondingly intractable
when required to represent a realization from which it is
separated by its very concreteness. This defect resembles
the defect of the beta-element as an element in thinking.
The transformation which the model has to undergo to permit of its employment as a generalization is analogous to the
process by which sense data are transformed into alpha-
elements. The alternative to finding or making a new model
is to resort to further abstraction. The model is then replaced
by the Scientific Deductive System. As an example of the
issues involved I shall take the scientific approach to the
problems of the K relationships.

CHAPTER TWENTY-SIX

1. The terms Love, Hate and Knowing had precedent models. Link can imply a model or an abstraction. The failure of the patient to solve his problems may in some cases depend on the fact that he employs models wrongly. In making his own model the analyst needs in such cases to be aware of and to lay bare the model used by the patient. The analyst's model must be such that it enables him to arrive at an interpretation of the facts that present themselves for scrutiny. If the analyst supposes that the patient's thinking is at fault and is at the source of his troubles he will need a model and a theory of thinking of his own; he will need a model for the patient's mode of thinking and he will need to deduce from that what the patient's model for thinking is. He may then compare his model and abstraction with the patient's. The patient who thinks words are things-in-themselves does not feel he is doing the same thing as we think he is doing when we say he is thinking. To compare the ordinary view of thinking with such a patient's it is necessary to find a suitable model and theory. One model has, as we have seen, a wide-spread distribution, the model derived from the emotional experience of the digestive system. There is ordinarily no need to discard this model though its failings are obvious—it can still help to be able to speak of "undigested facts". But for a psycho-analytic investigation of thinking it is inadequate and some different model is needed. This need has become obvious in the psycho-analytic investigation of disorders of thought. Investigation of mental development shows that some individuals behave as if their model of thinking was not that of a healthy digestive system or perhaps of a digestive system at all. It is therefore necessary to discover what their model is.

2. Freud said thought provided a means for the restraint of motor discharge (Two Principles); it was no longer concerned with unburdening the mental apparatus of accretions of stimuli but was now employed in the appropriate altera-tion of reality. According to this, thought is a substitute for motor discharge although he does not say that motor discharge ceases to function as a method of disburdening the psyche of accretions of stimuli. But through projective identification thought itself takes on the function previously entrusted to motor discharge—namely ridding the psyche of accretions of stimuli; like "action" it may be directed to altering the environment, depending on whether the personality is directed to evasion of frustration or modification of it. "Thinking" can be regarded as the name given to a model or abstraction derived from a realization; with an actual patient the problem is to determine what he represents by the term thinking. An individual may mean that thoughts are being used and a thought is a not good breast, a "need for a breast" breast. The problem then would be to see how he uses this "object", particularly if the patient felt unable to evacuate it—to disburden himself of these accretions of internal stimuli.

3. The problem is simplified if "thoughts" are regarded as epistomologically prior to thinking and that thinking has to be developed as a method or apparatus for dealing with "thoughts". If this is the case then much will depend on whether the "thoughts" are to be evaded or modified or used as part of an attempt to evade or modify something else. If they are felt to be accretions of stimuli then they may be similar to or identical with beta-elements and as such would lend themselves to treatment by motor discharge and the operation of the musculature to effect the discharge. Talking therefore must be considered as potentially two different activities, one as a mode of communicating thoughts and the other as an employment of the *musculature* to disencumber the personality of thoughts.

4. An apparatus has to be produced to make it possible to think the already existing thought. As a "model" of thought I take a sensation of hunger that is associated with

a visual image of a breast that does not satisfy but is of a kind that is needed. This needed object is a bad object. All objects that are needed are bad objects because they tantalize. They are needed because they are not possessed in fact; if they were possessed there would be no lack. As they don't exist they are peculiar objects different from objects that exist. Thoughts then, or these primitive elements that are proto-thoughts, are bad, needed objects and to be got rid of because they are bad. They can be got rid of either by evasion or modification. The problem is solved by evacuation if the personality is dominated by the impulse to evade frustration and by thinking the objects if the personality is dominated by the impulse to modify the frustration. In analytic practice confusion and complication is produced for the analyst because both types of personality employ the same name for objects that are essentially dissimilar. The dissimilarity can be emphasized by comparison. If evasion dominates, the name denotes a beta-element, that is a thing-in-itself and not the name that represents it. The thing in itself is non-existent and therefore tantalizing. It is dealt with by divestment (evacuation). If modification dominates, the name denotes an alpha-element, that is the name is the name of the representation of a thing in itself. The name is of a thing in itself that exists and is therefore potentially available for use in achieving fulfilment. Further complication is produced because a patient is unlikely to be consistent and does not make clear what objects are being denoted by the names he is using.

5. If the patient cannot "think" with his thoughts, that is to say that he has thoughts but lacks the apparatus of "thinking" which enables him to use his thoughts, to think them as it were, the first result is an intensification of frustration because thought that should make it "possible for the mental apparatus to support increased tension during a delay in the process of discharge" is lacking. The steps taken by the patient to rid himself of the objects, the proto-thoughts or thoughts which to him are inseparable from frustration, have then led him to precisely the pass that he wished to avoid, namely to tension and frustration unalleviated by the capacity

for thought. The lack of a capacity for thought therefore implies a twofold failure. It is due to absence of alpha-elements and lack of apparatus to use alpha-elements if they exist. The double failure becomes significant in the psycho-analysis of the psychotic when the patient re-establishes alpha-function, and therefore his capacity for dreaming, and yet remains unable to think. He therefore resorts to projective identification as a mechanism for dealing with "thoughts". But if alpha-function has been developed there is a corresponding increase in dominance of reality principle and a corresponding change in projective identification which loses some of its quality of omnipotent phantasy and gains through the patient's ability to give it substance.

6. Clinically this shows itself in an increase in the patient of a sense of loss when he is speaking. The sense of loss appears to originate in an awareness that the thoughts being lost are good or valuable thoughts differing in this respect from beta-elements. The analyst likewise becomes aware of a change in the impact on himself of the patient's manipulations.

7. "Thinking", in the sense of engaging in that activity which is concerned with the use of thoughts, is embryonic even in the adult and has yet to be developed fully by the race. Quite conscious attempts are directed to this end. The problem is more accurately apprehended and investigated if it is seen to depend on (1) "thoughts" and (2) "thinking" which developed in response to the challenge presented by the existence of "thoughts". In the psycho-analysis of "disorders of thought", psycho-analytic investigation must be directed towards the development and nature of the "thoughts", alpha- and beta-elements, and then to the nature of the apparatus used for dealing with "thoughts". Only then can the investigation be devoted to what content or other factor contributed to the breakdown. The division into two classes and the attribution of priority to "thoughts" is subject to the limitations peculiar to the relationship existing in all scientific work between the realization and the representative theory to which it is believed to approximate. The division and priority are epistemologically and

logically necessary, that is to say the theory that thought is
prior to thinking is itself prior, .n the hierarchy of hypotheses
in the scientific deductive system, to the hypothesis of
thinking. A corresponding priority is epistemologically necessary in the realization corresponding to the theory of
thinking I have adumbrated here.

8. The scientific deductive system is called for because
the model made during the emotional experience which it
is intended to illuminate is not sufficiently abstract. Its
elements are derived from previous emotional experiences
through the operation, concurrently with the emotional
experience, of alpha-function. The model is formed by the
exercise of a capacity similar to that which is in evidence
when the two eyes operate in binocular vision to correlate
two views of the same object. The use in psycho-analysis
of conscious and unconscious in viewing a psycho-analytic
object is analogous to the use of the two eyes in ocular observation of an object sensible to sight. Freud attributed this
function, the sense organ of psychical quality, to consciousness alone. The scientific deductive system is elaborated
away from the emotional experience and is a conscious act
of construction in the course of which signs are chosen and
rules for their manipulation formulated. Can such a procedure be profitably adapted to the psycho-analytic investigation of the development of thoughts and the apparatus
that employs them? I shall answer the question by making
the attempt in my last chapter and incidentally summarizing
this book.

9. The first requisite for the use of a theory is proper
conditions for observation. The most important of these is
psycho-analysis of the observer to ensure that he has reduced
to a minimum his own inner tensions and resistances which
otherwise obstruct his view of facts by making correlation
by conscious and unconscious impossible. The next step
is for the analyst to bring his attention to bear. Darwin
pointed out that judgment obstructs observation. The
psycho-analyst however must intervene with interpretations
and this involves the exercise of judgment. A state of reverie
conducive to alpha-function, obtrusion of the selected fact,

and model-making together with an armoury limited to a few essential theories ensure that a harsh break in observation of the kind Darwin had in mind becomes less likely; interpretations can occur to the analyst with the minimum disturbance of observation.

10. The "selected fact", that is to say the element that gives coherence to the objects of the paranoid-schizoid position and so initiates the depressive position, does so by virtue of its membership of a number of different deductive systems at their point of intersection. Obtrusion of the selected fact is accompanied by an emotion such as is experienced in regarding the object in reversible perspective. The total process depends on relaxed attention; this is the matrix for abstraction and identification of the selected fact. From the model thus made and its matching with the realization a special theory, the psycho-analytic interpretation, must be abstracted. This abstraction involves the difference between a theory associated with a scientific deductive system and a psycho-analytic interpretation. The analyst has to concern himself with two models, one that he is called upon to make and the other implicit in the material produced by the patient.

11. I shall first consider the model that has to be made by the analyst. The model is produced by the analyst as a part of theory construction and is *not* itself an interpretation, except in the conversational sense of the term, of what is taking place. The relevant theory may be the Oedipus theory. The analyst must determine from the patient's material why he is producing it and what the correct interpretation should be. The model plays its part in the determination by enabling the analyst to match what the patient is actually saying, with the theory or theories known to psycho-analysis as the Oedipus complex. The model throws into relief two sets of ideas, those that relate to the patient's material and those that relate to the body of psycho-analytic theory.

12. Model making makes it possible to retain the structure of psycho-analytic theory without loss of the flexibility necessary to meet the moment to moment needs of

psychoanalytic practice. On the one hand the theory may become too set because of its concreteness and on the other open to endless proliferation because analysts, finding themselves in an impasse, may prefer to produce a new theory *ad hoc* rather than undergo the ardours of using existing theory properly. The advantage of the theory of functions and of the development of model making as an essential part of it, is that the analyst has plenty of scope for really satisfying himself, and therefore his patient, that it is the patient as a real man or woman whose affairs are under scrutiny and not just the supposed mental mechanisms of a dummy. At the same time the particularization necessary for this does not involve proliferating theories. The model makes it possible to find the correspondence between the patient's thinking and the main body of psycho-analytic theory by interpretations that are related closely both to theory and the statements and conduct of the patient. Model making thus increases the number of contingencies that can be met and decreases the number of psycho-analytic theories that the psycho-analyst needs as his working equipment. If every analyst set himself the task of producing a handbook of psycho-analytic theories to provide a foundation of the minimum number of premises from which a wide range of subsidiary theories could be deduced, I believe it would be possible with less than six major theories. Psycho-analytic virtue lies not in the number of theories the analyst can command but the minimum number with which he can meet any contingency he is likely to meet. The range of such theoretical equipment depends on the method of application and that on the procedure of model making. There will be less disposition to put forward new theories when none is called for if the distinction between model and theory is kept clear. The danger lies in being cramped by a theoretical system that is frustrating not because it is inadequate but because it is not being properly used.

CHAPTER TWENTY-SEVEN

THIS CHAPTER will be taken up with the construction of some theories that I have found serviceable. It is intended also to serve as an example of the use of the theory of functions and other ideas I have put forward and thus to take the place of a summary of the main items in the book.

THE K LINK

1. The theory of functions and alpha-function are not a part of psycho-analytic theory. They are working tools for the practising psycho-analyst to ease problems of thinking about something that is unknown.

2. The term "function", used in the sense of a function of the personality, has not the meaning it possesses for the mathematician or the mathematical logician though it has features partaking of the meaning of both. I propose it as a term for use in the practice of psycho-analysis; its full designation, if there is any doubt, is "psycho-analytic function of the personality" but otherwise it should be designated simply "function" and given the sign ψ. Alpha-function is a factor of ψ.

3. The term "factor" is the name of an element of any function. It may be represented by the unsaturated element (ξ) in $\psi\ (\xi)$ and there must be a realization approximating to it. What the realization is that satisfies it, in the mathematical sense of satisfying the terms of an equation, is a matter to be determined by the psycho-analytical investigation itself.

4. The theory of functions, and alpha-function in particular, does not diminish or increase existing psycho-analytical theories. In this it differs from the arguments that follow.

5. Melanie Klein has described an aspect of projective identification concerned with the modification of infantile fears; the infant projects a part of its psyche, namely its bad feelings, into a good breast. Thence in due course they are removed and re-introjected. During their sojourn in the good breast they are felt to have been modified in such a way that the object that is re-introjected has become tolerable to the infant's psyche.

6. From the above theory I shall abstract for use as a model the idea of a container into which an object is projected and the object that can be projected into the container: the latter I shall designate by the term contained. The unsatisfactory nature of both terms points the need for further abstraction.

7. Container and contained are susceptible of conjunction and permeation by emotion. Thus conjoined or permeated or both they change in a manner usually described as growth. When disjoined or denuded of emotion they diminish in vitality, that is, approximate to inanimate objects. Both container and contained are models of abstract representations of psycho-analytic realizations.

8. The next step in abstraction is dictated by the need for designation. I shall use the sign ♀ for the abstraction representing the container and ♂ for the contained.

9. These signs both denote and represent. They are variables or unknown in that they are replaceable. They are constants in that they are only replaceable by constants. For syntactical purposes they are functors.

10. Reconsidering K in the light of previous discussion although K is essentially a function of two objects it can be considered as a function of one.

The earliest and most primitive manifestation of K occurs in the relationship between mother and infant. As a part object relationship it may be stated as a relationship between mouth and breast. In abstract terms it is between ♂ and ♀ (as I have proposed the use of these signs).

In K, L and H being factors and therefore subordinate, ♂ is projected into ♀ and abstraction, of a type that I shall use the term commensal to describe, follows. By commensal I mean ♂ and ♀ are dependent on each other for mutual benefit and without harm to either. In terms of a model the mother derives benefit and achieves mental growth from the experience: the infant likewise abstracts benefit and achieves growth.

11. The activity that I have here described as shared by two individuals becomes introjected by the infant so that the ♂ ♀ apparatus becomes installed in the infant as part of the apparatus of alpha-function. A model is provided by the idea of the infant who explores an object by putting it into his mouth. What talking was originally done by the mother, possibly a rudimentary designatory function, is replaced by the infant's own baby talk.

12. Using 11 above as a model from which to abstract a theory to represent the realization of the development of thoughts, I propose the following terms: (*a*) Pre-conception. This term represents a state of expectation. The term is the counterpart of a variable in mathematical logic or an unknown in mathematics. It has the quality that Kant ascribes to an empty thought in that it can be thought but cannot be known.

(*b*) Conception. Conception is that which results when a pre-conception mates with the appropriate sense impressions. I have used a phrase in which the implied model is obvious. The abstraction from the relationship of pre-conception to sense impressions is ♀ to ♂ (NOT ♂ to ♀).

13. To summarize. The relationship between mother and infant described by Melanie Klein as projective identification is internalized to form an apparatus for regulation of a pre-conception with the sense data of the appropriate realization. This apparatus is represented by a model: the mating of pre-conception with sense-impressions to produce a conception. The model is in turn represented by ♂ ♀.

14. The repetition of mating of pre-conception and sense data, that results in commensal abstraction, promotes growth in ♂ and ♀. That is to say the capacity for taking in sense impressions develops together with the capacity for awareness of sense data. Growth of ♂ and ♀ can be represented pictorially by models described in 16 and 17 below.

15. For the model for the growth of ♀ I shall borrow Elliott Jaques concept of the reticulum. (In doing so I do not propose alterations in his concept or claim that my use is justified by the intrinsic qualities of the concept. The relationship of his concept to my use of it as a model must be determined in the course of the development of psychoanalysis.) The model I propose is as follows:

♀ develops by accretion to produce a series of sleeves that are conjoined. The result is a reticulum in which the gaps are the sleeves and the threads forming the meshes of the reticulum are emotions. Borrowing from Tarski (*Introduction to Logic:* Oxford 1956 page 5) his simile of the questionnaire with blanks that have to be filled in, the sleeves can be likened to the blanks in the questionnaire. The structure of the questionnaire has as its counterpart the connecting threads of the reticulum.

16. The model for the growth of ♂ is a medium in which lie suspended the "contents". The "contents" must be conceived of as protruding from a base which is unknown. A two-dimensional image is provided by the parabola. The medium in a commensal relationship of ♂ and ♀ is tolerated doubt. That is to say that the developing ♂ can be visualized as being similar to the elements of the paranoid-schizoid position but without the sense of persecution. It is the state described by Poincaré, and quoted by me, as one in which elements are not seen to cohere.

17. Stating 15 & 16 above abstractly we have on the one hand (♀ ≠ ♀ + ♀. . .) and on the other (♂. ♂. ♂. . . .) where the + signs represent variables replaceable by signs representing emotions and . signs represent a constant representing doubt.

18. Growing ♂ ♀ provides the basis of an apparatus for learning by experience. Reconsideration of paras 5 to 17 shows that from thoughts and the development of thoughts there arises the apparatus for thinking the thoughts. I shall now consider the nature and operation of that apparatus. It cannot have the rigid clear-cut structure this attempt at exposition implies partly because the attempt is a clarification and partly because I have to use for something animate

terms such as apparatus and structure. I shall denote the growing ♂ ♀ by using the signs ♂^{n} and ♀^{n}. The signs have no logical significance but are intended merely to save time.

19. Learning depends on the capacity for ♀^{n} to remain integrated and yet lose rigidity.[1] This is the foundation of the state of mind of the individual who can retain his knowledge and experience and yet be prepared to reconstrue past experiences in a manner that enables him to be receptive of a new idea. Using this last statement as a model from which to abstract, the elements (♀) of ♀^{n} must be held by a constant $+$ that is capable of replacement, in other words it must function as a variable. Only then can it represent an apparatus capable of changing emotion. On the replacement of one emotion, represented by $+$, by another emotion, also represented by $+$, does the capacity for re-formation, and therefore receptivity, of ♀^{n} depend. Similarly the penetrability of ♂ elements in ♂^{n} depends on the value of ".". The value of "$+$" and "." is determined by the same factor, namely emotion and the emotion is a function of the personality.

20. Hitherto I have been describing a type of abstraction I have named commensal in which the link between objects is commensal. K has depended on that type of link between objects through all the phases of mental activity and growth. Since "$+$" and "." represent emotions it is evident that we need to know what emotions are compatible with a commensal relationship and therefore with K. The problem will receive some illumination in my next chapter in which I discuss $-$ K.

21. The pattern ♂ ♀ represents an emotional realization associated with learning that becomes progressively more complex as it constantly recurs throughout mental development. This growing and recurring event, represented by ♀^{n} ♂^{n}, I shall attempt to clarify by depicting one of its aspects, in its more developed and sophisticated stages, by a more sophisticated description.

♀^{n} represents a late stage in a series of stages that commences with a few relatively simple undifferentiated preconceptions probably related to feeding, breathing and excretion.

22. The abstractions from the commensal mating of ♀

with ♂ include the formation of words that are names for various hypotheses stating that certain sense data are constantly conjoined. From such relatively simple beginnings the ♀^{n} ♂^{n} abstracts successively more complex hypotheses and finally whole systems of hypotheses which are known as scientific deductive systems. These extremely complex systems though hardly recognizable in their origins nevertheless retain the receptive qualities denoted by ♀. The phenomena related to realizations multiply as the realizations, though limited to the progress in experience of one man, are yet multiplied enough to reveal an expanding universe to which presumably an expanding realization corresponds. ♂^{n} must therefore have a phenomenological counterpart represented by the concept of infinity.

The elements of the many scientific deductive systems must be capable of recombination—the use of an hypothesis from one deductive system as premiss in a different deductive system is a familiar example. On the theory put forward here the freedom necessary for these recombinations depends on emotions suffusing the psyche because these emotions are the connective in which the scientific deductive systems and the elements of ♂^{n} are embedded. Tolerance of doubt and tolerance of a sense of infinity are the essential connective in ♂^{n} if K is to be possible.

CHAPTER TWENTY-EIGHT

− K

1. SOME PATIENTS who are concerned to prove their superiority to the analyst by defeating his attempts at interpretation can be shown that they are mis-understanding the interpretations to demonstrate that an ability to mis-understand is superior to an ability to understand. Interpretations based on this insight can lead to further development of the analysis. If the patient suffers from a disorder of thought, interpretations of mis-understanding lead to some illumination, but do not appear to carry matters much further. For this problem a more inclusive concept is necessary.

2. Using the procedures adumbrated here I first resort to the abstraction represented by the sign K and then reverse the sign to − K. Assuming that the signs of all factors in K are also reversed, I use the theories that represent factors in K as preconceptions to aid in my search for factors in − K. Those factors, now employed as pre-conceptions are employed, can be represented in their new employment by ♀. It may make my meaning clearer if I say that I am in a state of receptive observation as opposed to a state in which I pass judgment on what I observe. I can further describe it approximately by saying I become absorbed in my task of observation or that I am absorbed in the facts. In short there are many ways in which I can attempt to describe my mental activity; all of them may contribute to an understanding of what I am engaged on, but none of them does so with the precision that I think necessary for communicating psycho-analytic procedure. The advantage of employing a sign ♀ to designate the new role of factors in K is that it at least indicates

95

that the reader's comprehension of my meaning should contain an element that will remain unsatisfied until he meets the appropriate realization, an element that can be represented by the sign ψ (ξ), (ξ) being itself the sign for an unsaturated element.

3. The sections that follow are an attempt to describe the results of observation in which preconceptions are harnessed to the task of discovery and not treated as predilections to be eliminated if possible—for that is in any case not possible.

4. Inevitably one wonders at various points in the investigation why such a phenomenon as that represented by — K should exist. The answer to that question must be sought in psycho-analytic work with individual patients. I shall consider one factor only—Envy. By this term I mean the phenomenon described by Melanie Klein in *Envy and Gratitude*.

5. I have described the role of projective identification in K as a commensal relationship between ♀ and ♂. In — K, as exemplified in a patient represented by the sign ψ (ξ) in whom preliminary investigation reveals Envy as likely to be one of the factors needed to satisfy (ξ), the relationship of ♀ to ♂ is represented by ♀ + ♂ where + can be replaced by Envy. Using this formulation to represent infant and breast (to resort to less abstract signs) and using as a model an emotional situation in which the infant feels fear that it is dying, the model I construct is as follows: the infant splits off and projects its feelings of fear into the breast together with envy and hate of the undisturbed breast. Envy precludes a commensal relationship. The breast in K would moderate the fear component in the fear of dying that had been projected into it and the infant in due course would re-introject a now tolerable and consequently growth-stimulating part of its personality. In — K the breast is felt enviously to remove the good or valuable element in the fear of dying and force the worthless residue back into the infant. The infant who started with a fear he was dying ends up by containing a nameless dread.

6. The violence of emotion that is associated with Envy, and can be one of the factors in the personality in which — K

is in evidence, affects the projective processes so that far
more than the fear of dying is projected. Indeed it is as if
virtually the whole personality was evacuated by the infant.
The process of denudation described in 5 is therefore more
serious, because more extensive, than is implied in the simple
example of the projection of a fear of dying. The seriousness
is best conveyed by saying that the will to live, that is
necessary before there can be a fear of dying, is a part of the
goodness that the envious breast has removed.

7. Since the projection by the infant is also impelled by
envy the projection is felt as an envious denudation of the
psyche from which, in K, only the fear of dying would have
been removed. There is therefore hardly any infant to
re-introject or into whom the denuded fear of dying can be
forced. In K, ♀ ♂ can find a habitat because the infant can
re-introject the related pair. But — ♀ and — ♂ are returned
to an object that covers them with little more than the
semblance of a psyche.

8. The object that I described as being re-introjected as
♀ ♂ in K was one in which the relationship of the elements
♀ and ♂ was commensal. In — K it is envious and therefore
it is necessary to consider — ♀ and — ♂ and — (♀ ♂) in
more detail. There are a number of peculiar features that
are difficult to reconcile in a coherent theory. I shall
accordingly describe them first without any attempt at
explanation.

9. In the first place its predominant characteristic I can
only describe as "without-ness". It is an internal object
without an exterior. It is an alimentary canal without a
body. It is a super-ego that has hardly any of the characteristics of the super-ego as understood in psycho-analysis: it
is "super" ego. It is an envious assertion of moral superiority
without any morals. In short it is the resultant of an envious
stripping or denudation of all good and is itself destined to
continue the process of stripping described in 5, as existing,
in its origin, between two personalities. The process of
denudation continues till — ♂ — ♀ represent hardly more
than an empty superiority-inferiority that in turn degenerates
to nullity.

10. In so far as its resemblance to the super-ego is concerned — (♀ ♂) shows itself as a superior object asserting its superiority by finding fault with everything. The most important characteristic is its hatred of any new development in the personality as if the new development were a rival to be destroyed. The emergence therefore of any tendency to search for the truth, to establish contact with reality and in short to be scientific in no matter how rudimentary a fashion is met by destructive attacks on the tendency and the reassertion of the "moral" superiority. This implies an assertion of what in sophisticated terms would be called a moral law and a moral system as superior to scientific law and a scientific system.

11. Restating 10 in other terms, it can be seen as implying an attempt to retain a power to arouse guilt as an essential capacity. The power to arouse guilt is essential and appropriate to the operation of projective identification in a relationship between infant and breast. This guilt is peculiar in that its association with primitive projective identification implies that the guilt is meaningless. The — (♀ ♂) contrasts therefore with conscience in that it does not lend itself to constructive activity.

12. In contrast with the learning (K) function of ♀ ♂, — (♀ ♂) is engaged in the collection of meaningful ♂ elements for subjection to — ♀ so that these elements are stripped of their meaning and only the worthless residue is retained. The analyst's interpretations are a part of the ♂ elements that are so treated, with the result that they are denuded of meaning. This envious extraction is to be contrasted with the process of abstraction peculiar to ♀ ♂ in K. The ego-like function of — ♀ ♂ is unlike ego function in destroying rather than promoting knowledge. This destructive activity is tinged with "moral" qualities derived from the "super"-ego quality of — (♀ ♂). In other words — ♀ ♂ asserts the moral superiority and superiority in potency of *UN*-learning.

13. Successful operation of — (♀ ♂) has as its achievement growth in development and power of — ♀ and an ever-increasing accretion of ♂ elements for conversion to — ♂ elements. In other words alpha-elements, however obtained,

are acquired for conversion to beta-elements. In practice it means that the patient feels surrounded not so much by real objects, things-in-themselves, but, by bizarre objects that are real only in that they are the residue of thoughts and conceptions that have been stripped of their meaning and ejected.

14. The relationship of K to − K can be epitomized by saying that in K particularization and concretization of the abstract and general is possible, but in − K it is not because the abstract and general, in so far as they exist, are felt to become things-in-themselves. Conversely in K the particular can be generalized and made abstract, but in − K the particular becomes denuded of any quality it has; denudation not abstraction is the end product.

15. Finally, though I shall not follow it up here, the theories in which I have used the signs K and − K can be seen to represent realization in groups. In K the group increases by the introduction of new ideas or people. In − K the new idea (or person) is stripped of its value, and the group in turn feels devalued by the new idea. In K the climate is conducive to mental health. In − K neither group nor idea can survive partly because of the destruction incident to the stripping and partly because of the product of the stripping process.

NOTES

1.5.1. The term "realization" is used in the sense that it has if it is said that Euclidean geometry of three dimensions has the structure of ordinary space as one of its realizations. The expression is used in an easily comprehensible way in *Algebraic Projective Geometry*, Semple and Kneebone (O.U.P., 1956), Chapter 1, where the concept of geometry is discussed.

1.5.2. The term "deductive system", or "scientific deductive system", is used to cover any approximation to, or projected approximation to, the logical systems described in *Scientific Explanation*, Braithwaite (C.U.P., 1955), Chapter II and onwards.

1.7.1. Compare: *The Logic of Scientific Discovery*, K. R. Popper (Hutchinson, 1959), p. 35, note 2, where the difficulty is admirably illustrated.

2.1.1. *Two Principles of Mental Functioning* S. Freud. (C.P., 1911, Vol. IV), The quotations and references in this chapter, being intended to indicate the limits of the area in which I wish to use the concept of alpha-function are not selected with the rigour that I consider necessary if the selection is made for use in a scientific theory or as a factor for use with the theory of functions.

2.2.1. S. Freud (1954), *Interpretation of Dreams*, p. 615.

2.3.1. S. Freud, *Two Principles of Mental Functioning* (C.P.), Chapter IV, p. 15.

2.5.1. Notes on Some Schizoid Mechanisms, M. Klein, *Developments in Psycho-analysis*, p. 300.

2.5.2. M. Klein, *Ibid.*, p. 293.

2.5.3. Importance of Symbol Formation in the Development of the Ego. M. Klein, *Contributions to Psycho-analysis*, p. 236.

2.5.4. Differentiation of Psychotic from the non-psychotic Personalities. W. R. Bion.

3.2.1 and 2. I use the term "phenomena" to cover what Kant called secondary and primary qualities. The term "things-in-themselves" I hold with Kant to refer to objects that are unknowable to mankind.

5.1.1. The term 'envy' is here used to describe generally the phenomena described in detail by Melanie Klein in *Envy and Gratitude*.

5.2.1. *See* 4.4.

5.3.1. W. R. Bion, "The Differentiation of Psychotic from non-psychotic Personalities." *Int. J. of Psycho-analysis*.

5.3.2. *See* 6.2.

7.3.1. "Differentiating conscious from unconscious." This use of terms is typical of the difficulty of using ambiguous terms when no more precise terms are available. I do not mean "the" conscious or "the" unconscious because that would imply that an observer would be required to differentiate two objects. Yet I do not wish to exclude that shade of meaning because when elements have been differentiated, some becoming conscious and some unconscious, it is reasonable to say there is an unconscious if such a concept is valuable.

10.1.1. This suggests a capacity for intuition that seems incompatible with ordinary ideas of insanity. In so far as it is purposive conduct the purpose must be controlled and dictated by the non-psychotic part of the personality.

The evocation peculiar to the beta-screen, if successful,

means that the patient is starved of genuine therapeutic material, namely truth, and therefore those of his impulses that are directed to survival are overworked attempting to extract cure from therapeutically poor material.

10.2.1. The reversal of direction is compatible with the treatment of thoughts by evacuation; that is to say that if the personality lacks the apparatus that would enable it to "think" thoughts but is capable of attempting to rid the psyche of thoughts in much the same way as it rids itself of accretions of stimuli, then reversal of alpha-function may be the method employed.

10.2.2. The stripping of alpha-elements of the characteristics that differentiate them from beta-elements is important. A model is provided by the theory of the word as the name of a scientific deductive system, e.g. "Dada". The scientific deductive system consists of a series of hypotheses. The system is a statement that certain elements are constantly conjoined. The conjunction and the elements conjoined depend upon the pre-conception (*a priori* knowledge of the individual) and the realizations that have been found by the individual successively to approximate to the preconception and transform it into a conception. The conception in turn becomes an abstraction, or model, to which still more realizations are believed or found to approximate. It is these associations, now stated by the scientific deductive system to be conjoined constantly, (and by the fact of that statement *are* constantly conjoined in the mind of the individual) that are stripped from the word that is the name of the scientific deductive system so that finally only the name "Dada" remains. I am not considering the social value of the name "Dada" nor yet the social version of the scientific deductive system called by that name. The aspect I am discussing is that which exists before publication and is therefore private to the individual. It is that aspect of a phenomenon that would, in Kant's terms, be called secondary quality unless there was evidence, through publication, of the universality that Kant attributes to the primary qualities.

12.6.1. It would be impossible to proceed if I drew the reader's attention to the many instances where I myself am using phrases in which a model is implied rather than explicitly employed. Yet it may help in the elucidation of the problem with which I am concerned if I introduce such an interpretation occasionally as I do here. The term "welfare" itself suggests that mental development like physical development depends on the efficient

working of a mental alimentary system. Similarly development may suggest an externalization opposed to envelopment
that suggests internalization. One reader may be unconsciously
affected by the term welfare, because of the effect of concretization inherent in the implied model, though the theory was not
one with which he sympathized. On the other hand he might
not be effected at all by the model implicit in "development".
Readers of Fowler "The King's English" will be familiar with
the problem as it presents itself to one concerned with writing
good English (*see* his comments on metaphor in Chapter III).
No one would accuse Fowler of treating the writing of good
English lightly: yet he discusses this problem under the heading
of "Airs and Graces". For the practising psycho-analyst it lies
very near the root (or source, or matrix) of the problems of
capacity to think and to communicate thought which in turn
relate to the possibility or otherwise of achieving any real
knowledge.

12.7.1. The term "breast" is used for the concept employed by
Melanie Klein.

12.8.1. This idea may be compatible with Freud's statement
(Interpretation of Dreams, p. 602) of the primary process.

12.12.1. "Containing." I accept the implied model of a container in this and other passages in which it is necessary to use
terms such as "internal" or "external" objects. The model is
one I employ with reluctance as I think it is more appropriate
to immature than mature scientific thinking. Yet the nature
of this work and the lack of a language adequate for a scientific
approach to it compels the employment of models sometimes
known and more often suspected to be inappropriate, but
unavoidable because there is none better.

12.12.2. "bad breast." One of the problems of methodology with
which I am attempting to deal is illustrated here, and instances
of the same kind are plentiful in these pages: I shall not however mark them, leaving the reader to use his indulgence to
remedy the faults in exposition.

If I am asked what I mean by "bad breast" I can only say I
mean what the baby means. If I am asked what that is I can
say that in the course of the empirical experience of analysis
a patient shows certain feelings that I believe he has successfully
communicated to me. I must, for reasons connected with the
practice of analysis, say what those feelings are. To do so I
can fall back on certain material, the source of which I describe

later, to make a model. I compare this model with what is
taking place in the room and I make my interpretation that
amongst things the patient feels that he contains is a "bad
breast". I can present the view, as I see it, of infant and analyst
thus: A. I think the baby is having an unpleasant emotional
experience. B. I think the baby thinks it contains a bad breast.
A. I think the painful emotional experience is associated with
the coming together of a pre-conception and a beta-element.
B. Depending on the personality of the baby I think the baby
can: (1) eject the beta-element and lay the foundation for
incapacity to think (2) accept the beta-element with juxta-
position with the pre-conception, tolerate the intrinsic frustration, and thus be in process of alpha-function and the production of alpha-elements. I deal with the problem of pre-conceptions in my chapter on definitory hypotheses. In the practice
of analysis of patients with disorders of thought the analyst
requires, if possible, to establish a methodological framework
for himself but, and this is the crux of the matter, he must also
try to form some idea of what the infant thinks a feeling is.
For in disorders of thought it is obvious that some problem of
this kind has arisen in the infant's life and has not been solved.
Yet it is but a short step from this point to the absurdity of
attributing to the infant ideas, thoughts, concepts about what
the grown up calls a "feeling" that would do credit to a Kant.
Perhaps the answer is that only a Kant has such problems and
can solve them. Those who are not Kant either (*a*) do not have
these problems or (*b*) have these problems and develop disorders of thought.

13.1.1. What this means in practice is dealt with in the discussion
of the anthology of theories. Some idea of the magnitude of the
problem can be gained by a study of J. O. Wisdom's paper
"A Methodological Approach to the Problem of Hysteria"
(given to the Dutch Society for Psycho-Analysis, Amsterdam,
16th December 1957).

18.3.1. It is important to distinguish between the natures of the
two theories. The theory of alpha-function is introduced to
make it possible for the analyst to work without proposing a
new theory prematurely: Freud's theory of consciousness as
a sense organ for psychic quality is a part of recognized psycho-
analytic theory. *See* Chapter 18.

19.1.1. The process that the analyst is activating is, in the cases
in which he is investigating disorders of thought, designed to

investigate the same process in the patient. What psycho-analysts call phantasies are, in some cases at least, the present day survivals of what were once models that the patient formed to match his emotional experiences. In this respect the Oedipus myth is the survival of a model designed to match an infant emotional experience. If the case exhibits a disorder of thought it will be found that this model was never properly formed. As a result the oedipal situation will appear to be imperfectly developed or non-existent. Analysis of such a patient will reveal attempts, if the analysis is progressing, to formulate such a model.

See also Frege *Grundgesetze*, Vol. 1, p. 3. Geach-Black translations, p. 154, in which he discusses the concept that is, as it were, unsaturated.

19.2.1. To postulate such objects is open to the objection expressed by Frege against postulating Logical Objects, pp. 55, 56, *Grundlagen der Arithmetik*. The psycho-analyst must rely on the emotional experience of the analysis to reveal elements that he regards as factors of alpha-function. If he thinks that some of these factors merit description as analogues of sense impressions of concrete objects, it will be time to formulate the appropriate definitory hypotheses or to assign to them already exisiting terms that appear to be the names of such definitory hypotheses.

The analyst is therefore in the position of one, who, thanks to the power of "binocular" perception and consequent correlation that possession of a capacity for conscious and unconscious thought confers, is able to form models and abstractions that serve in elucidating the patient's inability to do the same.

More detailed description of this belongs to a description of clinical psycho-analysis into which I cannot enter here except in so far as it is incidental to illustrating my theme, namely the analyst's problem of method in learning by experience.

19.3.1. S. Freud, *Interpretation of Dreams*, Chapter VII B.

19.4.1. A process similar to that whereby pre-conception and experience of a realization are matched to stimulate the genesis of a conception.

20.7.1. The significance of this phenomenon alters with the emotion accompanying the experience. The patient may believe his activity is an evacuation but the nature of the belief depends on whether he is feeling aggressive, depressed or persecuted. If his activity is what the analyst regards as a normal verbal communication the patient does not know "what he is feeling". Superficially the patient's behaviour closely resembles a dream state such as I have described in 9.4. It is in fact a β-screen and cannot effect separation of thoughts into conscious and unconscious. If it were true dream the clinical situation would afford evidence of separation of conscious from unconscious such as exists when the patient is identified with unconscious and the analyst with conscious or vice versa.

21.3.1. *See* 22.8.

22.1.1. *See* R. E. Money-Kyrle, *Man's Picture of his World*, Chapter IV. The problem discussed in his book is essentially the same as that discussed here in the restricted field of psychoanalytic method. Money-Kyrle shows that it confronts everyman in the tasks he faces throughout his life.

22.2.1. *See* H. Rosenfeld On Drug Addiction, *Int. J. of Psycho-Anal.*, Vol. XLI, p. 472, for an illuminating instance of the problem I have illustrated by the model of the infant use of "Dada". Although it is reported as occurring in a dream it is typical of an attitude of mind not restricted to sleep.

22.3.1. Kant, *Critique of Pure Reason*. Translated by N. Kemp Smith, B XXVII–XXVIII, Preface to Second Edition.

22.6.1. H. Segal, Notes on Symbol Formation, *Int. J. of Psycho-Anal.* 1957. With regard to concretization and abstraction see her comments on equation.

23.1.1. H. Poincaré. *Science and Method*. (Dover Publications).

24.1.1. *See* J. O. Wisdom, A Methodological Approach to Problem of Hysteria, *Int. J. of Psycho-Anal.*, Vol. XLII. Also An Examination of the Psycho-Analytical Theories of Melancholia.

27.19.1 Elliott Jaques, Disturbances in the Capacity to Work, *Inst. J. of Psycho-Anal.*, Vol. XLI, 1960. It seems to me that the process of lysis and scanning, as Elliott Jaques describes it, depends on the existence of a system of preconceptions that can be brought to bear on the incoherent elements of the paranoid-schizoid position. Highly developed scientific investigation appears to me to employ theories, or scientific deductive systems, as the tool through which the counterpart of scanning is effected.

INDEX

Abstraction,
and formalization, mislead if
premature, 52
as means of correlation, 50
clinical instances of, 60–61
excessive, use of model to prevent
81
reapplied when a realization
approximates to it, 60
Alpha-elements,
description of, 46
failure to form, disastrous to
personality, 42
necessary for storage and dream
thoughts, 6
their ordering, 17
to prevent disturbance of conscious by the unconscious,
15
Alpha-function,
analogous with digestion, 35
and transformation of emotional
experience, 59
as an unknown, 38, 39
defined, 25
effects of attacks on, 9
failure of, confuses objective and
subjective, 59
its relation to *attention*, 5
its relation to *notation*, 5
related to attacks on linking, 21,
22
related to inability to sleep or
wake, 7
related to mother's capacity for
reverie, 36
reversal of, 25
substituted for theory of primary
and secondary processes,
54
use of, as an unknown, 3

Alpha-function (*contd.*)
works on emotional experience
occurring in waking or
sleeping, 6
Ambiguity, deliberate, of terms
used, viii
Anal-erotism, ineffectual interpretations of, 20
Attacks on linking, related to projective identification of conscious, 21
Attention,
Freud on, 5
related to model, 74

Beta-elements,
accorded chronological priority
to alpha-elements 35
and "ridding the psyche of
accretions of stimuli"
(*Freud*), 7
and undigested facts, 7
as things in themselves, 6
contrasted with bizarre objects,
25
defects of, similar to defects of
model, 81
evacuation of, by movements of
musculature, 13
evacuation of, forestalls alpha-
function, 35
not distinguished from an
evacuation, 59
produced by denudation, 99
related to acting-out, 6
screen of, 22, 23, 24
Bizarre objects,
associated with greed and failure
of satisfaction, 11
contrasted with beta-elements,
25, 58

THE GRID

	Defini-tory Hypo-theses 1	ψ 2	Nota-tion 3	Atten-tion 4	Inquiry 5	Action 6	... n.
A β-elements	A1	A2				A6	
B α-elements	B1	B2	B3	B4	B5	B6	... Bn
C Dream Thoughts Dreams, Myths	C1	C2	C3	C4	C5	C6	... Cn
D Pre-conception	D1	D2	D3	D4	D5	D6	... Dn
E Conception	E1	E2	E3	E4	E5	E6	... En
F Concept	F1	F2	F3	F4	F5	F6	... Fn
G Scientific Deductive System		G2					
H Algebraic Calculus							